10

Classroom in Conflict

SUNY Series, The Philosophy of Education
Philip L. Smith, editor

Classroom in Conflict
Teaching Controversial Subjects in a Diverse Society

John A. Williams

State University of New York Press

Published by
State University of New York Press, Albany

© 1994 State University of New York

For information, address State University of New York Press,
State University Plaza, Albany, NY 12246

Production by Cynthia Tenace Lassonde
Marketing by Bernadette LaManna

Excerpt from "An Event" in *Things of This World*, copyright © 1956 and
renewed 1984 by Richard Wilbur, reprinted by permission of Harcourt Brace
& Company.

Excerpt from "In Broken Images" from *Collected Poems 1975* by Robert
Graves. Copyright © 1975 by Robert Graves. Reprinted by permission of
Oxford University Press, Inc. and by permission of A. P. Watt, Ltd., on
behalf of the Trustees of the Robert Graves Copyright Trust.

"Friends in our questions," is reprinted from Josephine Miles, *Kinds of
Affection*, copyright 1967 by Josephine Miles, Wesleyan University Press
reprinted by permission of the University Press of New England. "Paths"
is reprinted from *Collected Poems, 1930–1983*, by Josephine Miles.
Josephine Miles 1983. University of Illinois Press. Used by permission of
the publisher.

Library of Congress Cataloging-in-Publication Data

Williams, John A., 1935–
    Classroom in conflict: teaching controversial subjects in a
diverse society/John A. Williams.
       p. cm. — (SUNY series the philosophy of education)
    Includes bibliographical references and index.
    ISBN 0-7914-2119-8 (HC: acid-free paper).
    ISBN 0-7914-2120-1 (PB: acid-free paper).
    1. College teaching—Social aspects—United States—Case studies.
2. Educational sociology—United States—Case studies.   3. Cultural
pluralism—United States—Case studies.   4. History—Study and
teaching (Higher)—Social aspects—United States.   I. Title.
II. Series: SUNY series in philosophy of education.
LB2331.W47   1994
378.1'25—dc20
                                            93-42768
                                                CIP

To Brenda

Friends in our questions, we looked together
At several mysteries,
And argued at them long and lightly, whether
Their no or yes.

Now one of us is sure, another's question
Turns counterfeit,
Unnegotiable in a redemption
By if or yet.

Wish that the future in its mysterious motion
Will come and will
Bring sureness to us all in our devotion,
But though, but still.

Josephine Miles, *Collected Poems.*

Going out into the fields of learning,
We shake the dew from the grasses.
All is new.
The paths we make through the wet grasses shine
As if with light.

They go where we take them, where they go.
Slow wings unfold, scarcely any
Motion happens but our heavy seeking.
Ant labors, hopper leaps away; too early for the bee,
The spider's silk hypotheses unfold
Tenacious, tenable.

Josephine Miles, "Paths," *Collected Poems.*

Contents

Foreword *by William R. Taylor* — ix

Acknowledgments — xiii

Chapter 1. One Classroom: An Introduction — 1

Chapter 2. Conflicting Views of the Classroom Revolution — 17

Chapter 3. The Teacher's Pitch and the Student Audience — 29

Chapter 4. Insiders and Outsiders — 41

Chapter 5. The Colonizer and the Colonized — 53

Chapter 6. The Uses of Comparative History — 65

Chapter 7. Teaching a Racially Sensitive Subject — 81

Chapter 8. On Understanding the South African Freedom Struggle — 89

Chapter 9. Imperialism — 97

Chapter 10. Nationalism and Racism: The Keywords — 105

Chapter 11. Structures of Argument in African History — 119

Chapter 12. The Other: The Problem of Authenticity — 135

Chapter 13. The World Context of American Pluralism — 143

Chapter 14. Learning in the Pluralist Classroom — 149

Chapter 15. The Rules of Discussion — 163

Chapter 16. In Pursuit of Pluralism — 171

Bibliography — 181

Index — 199

Foreword

"This book is like a breath of fresh air," one reader of the manuscript commented. The attacks on higher education during the last decade, sometimes referred to as the "culture wars," have created uneasiness and confusion about the capability of our colleges and universities to meet the challenges of a changing society and still remain centers of serious learning, reflection, and cultural reevaluation. These attacks have been launched in abstract language and have left us with a series of alarming charges. They come from the left and the right, from inside and outside the academy, and they have resulted in confused indictments. In one view or another, the indictments go something like this: the American mind has been "closed," its functioning inhibited by a preoccupation with "political correctness," a squeamishness about broaching controversial subjects. Basic knowledge is regularly sidetracked in favor of ideological indoctrination by left-leaning professors. Traditional liberal arts are neglected in favor of "junk culture." Or, on the contrary, the liberal arts curricula in American colleges and universities focus upon canonical works that bear the bias of the dead white European males who created them. They do not address the urgent social issues that concern a multicultural society of the kind we have developed.

John A. Williams has given us not another critical polemic or reformist panacea but rather a cautionary tale focused upon his own teaching—and learning—experience. *Classroom in Conflict* is that rare thing: a user's manual for the college teacher that is also a philosophical contribution to education. In moments of reflection— and they are many—its insights illuminate our times. While Williams writes as a historian of Africa and of Third World countries, he has written a book any teacher of history—or any other subject in the liberal arts—will profit from reading. Indeed, parents or any others who wonder what goes on in the best college classrooms will find Williams's accounts fascinating. This is because he has chosen, unlike most of the controversialists, to focus on the classroom, much of the time his own classroom; his students; and his successes and failures in communicating with them.

Readers will be struck by the modest, reasonable tone of what follows. Williams's excursions through his classrooms do not directly confront the contentions of any group of critics. His inclination has been to pass them by with a generous nod to their good intentions. "I agree with all these positions," he notes cagily at one point, "and I agree with none of them." Nonetheless, the principal issues in the current debate do come up in these chapters; and some issues, such as Afrocentrism (the contention that western civilization originated in Africa rather than Greek antiquity), are dealt with devastatingly but not in the abstract. Williams is like a biologist who sees the world through the mutating cells in his laboratory. In his history classes he has succeeded in isolating certain assumptions, or what he calls "mindsets," that obstruct the ability of students to broaden their understanding of historical subjects.

For Williams, these student mindsets rather than the contentions of Culture Warriors are the enemy. He singles out these characteristic tics in student mentality one by one and illustrates how he comes to grips with them. His approach is to show the inadequacy of a particular mindset by working Socratically within a student's experience. Some of these obstructive beliefs, such as a belief in positivism, relativism, or a student's desire for closure or certainty, are probably characteristic of almost all college students. Whole chapters are devoted to these problematic *idées fixes*. Other stumbling blocks for his students, such as simplistic ideas of imperialism, racism, and the assumption that authoritative knowledge must come from insiders within a social subgroup, are more general to students in history or the social sciences. The second half of the book is devoted to his experience in helping his students become more flexible and responsive, more attuned to nuance and more concrete.

Williams brings to these discussions of classroom stratagems and tactics a most unusual breadth of spirit and a winning candor. His objective as a teacher, he makes clear, has not been to manipulate students into sharing his own views but to make students aware of their own. All of his classroom maneuvering is directed at actively involving them in thinking and expanding their consciousness of historical societies. One problem with positivism and the focus on authoritative factual knowledge, he points out, is a student's tendency to look to the teacher or the text for truth: to take notes rather than taking thought. A problem with relativism is the disengaged judgmental escape this stance provides for students to explain anomalous historical behavior by saying, "That's just the way they did it then." To counter such obstructions to understanding, he seems given to class presentations that underscore the difficulty of final judgment by subjecting his students to multiple points of view on a particular movement or event.

Behind these tactical discussions and presiding over them in a muted way is an important philosophical view of history and historical experience. The complexity and fluidity of historical experience, Williams believes, defies authoritative representation. While he professes a belief in what he calls Gandhian truth—a belief that truth exists but is unobtainable by any one person—he also feels that such truth necessarily eludes historians in search of it. This belief has led him to question the assumption that the only authoritative spokesperson for historical subgroup is a member of that subgroup. He maintains, on the contrary, that there are no real insiders. All historians and historical actors are in one way or another partially blinded by their limited experience. Every insider is in key ways a biased witness. As an Africanist, he points out, he is the ultimate outsider: a white Protestant male of New England ancestry assaying the historical experience of a continent that is predominantly black and non-Christian. "Being an outsider," he tells us, "is my profession, my inclination, my identity." Historical understanding, accordingly, comes from sallies into history, from seeking out multiple views of events, from making exacting comparisons of historical movements, and by combining careful analysis with interjections of imagination. Such historical understanding as we can obtain moreover offers no panaceas. Historical knowledge of itself cannot eliminate racism or ethnic conflict. It can only help explain how and why they occur when they do.

If these reflections summarized in this way seem pessimistic, Williams's argument is far from pessimistic. Understanding, partial and provisional as it is, he seems to be telling us, is humanity's best hope. Its formation through education is an active accomplishment, something that all of us, student and teacher alike, must do for ourselves. It may not move mountains or in itself change societies, but without it our future would be bleak indeed. Teaching, therefore, is itself an engagement in the real world. "My own activist project," Williams tells us, "is to defend scholarly values in a dangerous world!"—an aim that is elegantly implemented in the chapters that follow.

William R. Taylor

Acknowledgments

It was my colleague for one year long ago, Peter Cline, who first suggested I write something based on my courses. Perhaps he did not mean quite this book, but the idea nestled in the back of my mind.

Another source of stimulus is the many sharp and curious students I get year after year. I started my career with students such as Robert C. Rutherford, Karen Nelson, and Janice Palmer at the University of Washington. These students made my career choice seem correct, and hundreds more followed—I recall especially the valuable discussions with Kwaku Amoabeng, Carrie Clark, Mary Lou Coker, Davin Fortuna, Blaine Gaustad, Darryl Hold, Harriet Jackson, Maloey Jones, Jerry Lannigan, Carrol Lasker, Tim McLaughlin, Michael Miner, Sandra Mohammed, Themba Ntinga, Dan Romanelli, Annie Sauter, Hank Shaw, Mrinalini Sinha, and John Sparks. I drew on Tom Beal's editorial skills to good effect. I have also received valuable criticisms and comments on the manuscript from Professors Jyoti Grewal of Luther College, Vincent Carey of SUNY Plattsburgh, and Marc Stern of Bentley College—all former Stony Brook students. There are scores of other students I would like to name; I cannot name them all.

The History Department at Stony Brook is an extraordinarily colleaguial place. Here is a built-in panel of experts, and all I have to do to check on almost any facet of knowledge is walk down the hall and knock at the appropriate door. The third floor of Stony Brook's Social and Behavioral Science Building is, in short, a superb academic environment, even though the State of New York heats and cools us with a stupefying intensity and inundates us with paper, which occasionally bears important messages.

William R. Taylor's help has been especially important: teaching with him stimulated my ideas, his encouragement helped me to get them on paper, and his many suggestions and criticisms helped me to improve what I had written.

Fred Weinstein has also given consistent encouragement, suggestions that have helped me to reexamine my facile assumptions and to realize what I was trying to say when I had not clearly said it. Joel Rosenthal's comments on these essays, and, generally, running conversation over the years, have also been invaluable. Bernard Semmel, too, has given perceptive comments and criticisms, which seem like footnotes to our many discussions of history, politics, and social values over nearly twenty-five years. Eric and Marie Lampard have been consistently supportive and encouraging during these same years.

My associations with colleagues from other departments have also been important to me over the years. Of many I could name, I must single out Amiri Baraka and Irwin Kra for their quick and probing conversations during a committee assignment we shared. Participants in the Faculty Development Workshop on American Pluralism held at Stony Brook in June 1991 were very helpful. I presented earlier versions of chapters 8 and 13 at that gathering. The comments of Olufemi Vaughan and Jane Sugarman were illuminating, and I owe a couple of crucial ideas in chapter 13 to Tim Brennan. Exchanges with Carole Kessner and Robert Goldenberg have been consistently rewarding. Eli Seifman's imaginative and experimental approaches have also made me realize the value of thinking about teaching.

Some of my ideas go back, I am sure, to my years in the History Department at the University of Washington. I can no longer tell now which of these ideas originated in conversations with Thomas J. Pressly, Vernon Carstensen, Dauril Alden, Arthur Bestor, or other colleagues there. But I do remember that the conversations were crucial for someone just starting out.

Getting to meet some of those faculty who started *The History Teacher* and signaled a new concern for teaching was also an encouragement. I think here of Glenn Linden, whose ideas about teaching history helped convince many historians across the country that teaching mattered. I met him during my Seattle years and also passed him down the line, in the course of the AHA History Education Project of the 1970s.

John Barell of Montclair State provided a professional's scrutiny to my discussion of teaching methods, for which I am grateful. Robert D. Marcus of SUNY Brockport gave the entire manuscript a thorough critical review. From Janet Ostercamp, I received valuable comments on two chapters. Thanks to these longtime friends.

The book has received a smooth sailing through the processes of publication at the State University of New York press, emerging in noticeably better shape than when it was submitted. I am grateful to Clay Morgan, the history editor; Cindy Lassonde, the production editor; Mary Beth Ray, the copy editor; and professor Philip L. Smith, in whose Philosophy of Education Series the book is appearing, for their support of this manuscript and their attention to the many details of producing a book. In time, I may even come to believe that the consistency, clarity, and correctness they provided was in my writing all along.

The majority of quoted passages in the book are passages of poetry, and this may occasion surprise in readers expecting a historian to quote historical writing. I never had the late Josephine Miles as a teacher, but I met her once at a poetry reading in 1958. I have found many of her poems to be succinct renderings of some of the ideas I was trying to present. The poem quoted at the beginning, "Friends in Our Questions," for example, brilliantly describes the best kind of classroom discussion. At times I almost fancied this book was an explanation of her poetry. None of the poetry here quoted is used simply to decorate the text. As I hope will be evident, all the poets quoted have probed deeply into language, meaning, and human experience. They are an important resource and stimulus to my thinking.

In the end, I am sure, the combined efforts of all of these students, friends, and colleagues could not save me from error, opacity, or confusion. I alone remain responsible for these faults in what follows.

1

One Classroom: An Introduction

Friend, these are the times
that reasons fail, straight lines,
credos and the clearest maps.

Mark Vinz, "Sleepwalking," *Climbing the Stairs.*[1]

I teach history to university students, and this book is about what goes on in my classroom. In the age of the culture wars, this is no longer the remote and obscure setting that it once seemed. In my classroom, as in thousands of others across the country, the student body is increasingly diverse. Related to this new diversity is an intense and potentially explosive political atmosphere. When controversial subjects enter the class—whether these are international conflicts, hotly debated political or social questions, or the clash of deeply held moral orientations or group identities—someone is likely to be offended, someone is likely to complain. The very possibility of discussing such matters in an atmosphere conducive to learning cannot be taken for granted. A class can break down, and the teacher is vulnerable to accusations that he or she has been insensitive or biased —serious charges in today's climate.

This book focuses throughout on the question of how we can teach, whether we can teach, such controversial subjects to today's students. The approach is informal and personal, with anecdotes drawn from my own classroom experience. These anecdotes are not meant simply as reminiscence or self-reflection but are used to provide a sociological view of the classroom. This is a way of countering the more abstract and theoretical, and more especially polemical, tone of many recent books about teaching.

The following chapters examine these problems from many different angles, resulting in a varied, even complex presentation, operating sometimes on several levels at once. But each of the approaches leads back to the central problem. The teacher, the students, the subject matter, and the medium of language itself, all enter into the analysis, not only in isolation but as they interact. The task here is to dissect and reconstitute the daily, practical processes of the classroom. To accomplish this, some passages will refer to the substantive material of my courses, drawing from, say, South African, West African, or New Zealand history for examples. Other sections then will raise pedagogical issues, proposing strategies designed to prevent conflict and breakdown. In this guise we look at the difficulties that now exist for arguing by comparison, developing critical reading skills, or framing rules of discussion. As well, conceptual discussions run through the chapters, with sections examining the difficulties of using and understanding words like *racism*, *nationalism* and *imperialism*.

However various the presentation in different parts of the book, the single task throughout is to show how teachers might create favorable conditions for free and open discussion, to open out a space where there will be, as Josephine Miles wrote,

> Coherence of agreement and difference,
> . . .
> To keep a precarious gritty life between chaos
> And bland entropy, in which we can prevail.
> Our mien of survival, to know our separate natures
> And allow them . . .
>
>   *Collected Poems.*[2]

For a few faculty members across the country, this has already proved impossible. They have found the personal costs of teaching controversial courses too high, and their personal decision has been to abandon them. That such decisions now so often seem necessary is a tragedy for higher education. The resulting sanitized education can only be a travesty. Certainly, such backing off would destroy my classroom. To find a way to engage such subjects without destroying the classroom in another way, through a clash of antagonistic opinions, is an urgent task.

The courses I teach are in history, and they often straddle the boundary between social sciences and humanities. I am especially interested in what students learn about the world beyond Europe and its interaction with an expanding Europe in modern times. Such subject matter implicates my classroom with some of the flash points of world conflict and academic controversy.

My own educational task rests on the belief that citizens of the United States do not know enough about the rest of the world, its cultures, histories, and languages. This inadequacy is especially glaring for Third World societies. Yet African, Asian, Pacific, Islamic, and Latin American societies are of increasing importance in our political and economic life. (Note here that I use the term *Third World* loosely and as a convenience. The term has no generally accepted, rigorous meaning, and debates about which societies are included or excluded, and on what grounds, are endless. I wish to bypass these debates and engage other matters.)

Education in these subjects has an important civic component. Such an education will help make democracy work better by making it more difficult to mislead the American public. In his American Historical Association Presidential address, speaking of graduate history education, Philip D. Curtin brought out the same point:

> Nor is our failure to help graduate students gain a world-historical perspective just of concern to the history departments that train them. What we teach passes to a broader public, and members of that public make political decisions that are crucial for us all. From the heights of power in the White House, we find portrayed a simplistic, tripartite division of the world into ourselves, our enemies, and the rest —who do not count, even though they form the vast majority of the world's population. (*American Historical Review,* LXXXIX (Feb 1984) 1)[3]

The conditions of the post Cold War world will certainly require a deeper and more nuanced knowledge of the Third World. Also, with increasing numbers of United States citizens coming from "the rest—who do not count," knowing about these areas becomes part of knowing ourselves.

To teach and study these subjects is to leap into controversy. They raise, after all, some of the most difficult political and moral issues of the contemporary world. Thus, one can expect that conflicts will occur in my classroom. Though they have not taken the extreme form that a few colleagues elsewhere have experienced, they have been disturbing enough, as for example:

- when a few students objected to an assigned book on African history, because it was not written by an African;
- when a student objected to the use of a historical document in class, because it contained racist language;
- when some students mistook illustrative quotations for my own views;
- and, more dramatically, when a fistfight almost broke out in class over a racist remark—This incident calls for a fuller account.

A few years ago, a white student, irritated at being contradicted in a class discussion, said that his critic, a black student, should shut up because he was inferior and had nothing to say worth listening to. The black student offered to fight. It was an electric moment and one I was ill-equipped to handle. My weak response was to divert the discussion and, generally, wish I could hide from the class in an imaginary hole in the floor. But a young woman in front said, "Are we really going to ignore what is being said? Why are we pretending nothing has happened?"

We took a break, and I convinced the black student that it was beneath his dignity to respond to or even to notice the opinions of someone he did not respect. In this I had the help of an older black student, whose career had given him rich experience in all sorts of situations.

The white student caught up with me after class. "They are inferior, aren't they?" he asked. "They have all the menial jobs. Why can't you say so?" I told him that superiority had to be earned by every individual, that the only possible reason to put down other people or groups was a lack of confidence in oneself, and that superior achievement earned through individual effort did not have to be claimed. I do not think I made much of an impression.

Another quite different and more recent incident also requires a full account. A student came up after class to discuss his own feelings about South Africa. He felt troubled. "I do not believe I am racist, and I believe black people should have opportunities," he said, "but I agree with the South African Conservative Party. They want to live in their own neighborhoods and have them to themselves—just like in my neighborhood. My neighborhood is all white, and we are not against black people, but we have a right to our own neighborhood.''

I did not blow up at him, call him racist, or denounce his views, as a secondary teacher said I should have done, when I related the incident to an adult evening class. I merely asked him whether a black family would be allowed their right to buy a house in this same neighborhood. That neighborhood, or ones like it, I conjectured, offered the best housing this family could afford. If one homeowner in the neighborhood sold to the black family, would the rest of the neighborhood accept the new neighbors?

"That would be a problem," said the student.

"Then isn't the black family being denied opportunity?" I asked.

That's all. I think the troubled student was merely more troubled. He was thinking about it. Perhaps he has continued thinking about it. The overt behavior of people discriminating in the housing market can, with difficulty, be regulated by law. Deeply held and often unexamined attitudes are not amenable to laws or to slogans.

I make no claim that I handled these incidents in an exemplary manner. I was unprepared for them, and my main reaction was probably embarrassment, my main motivation to avoid risk for myself. Perhaps I did help the students a little. I recall these experiences, really, because of their importance for me. Both these major incidents, and a host of minor ones, alerted me to the depth and complexity of prejudice and set me to examining my own approaches to teaching in today's changing environment.

My liberal code had been that all students are alike as students and that I should take no cognizance of their membership in different groups; that I should, if possible, not even notice that there are groups. However much this code once served as a rejection of older discriminatory practices, it is not adequate in today's conditions. It ignores the existence of strongly and positively held group identities, and it offers the teacher no assistance in the increasingly difficult task of communicating to today's diverse student body.

Nearly violent classroom breakdowns are, fortunately, very rare. But the little misunderstandings and difficulties of communication are ongoing daily occurrences. And to have a student come forward to talk about his private dilemmas is also unusual, but it may well be one sign of widespread bias. If so, here is a formidable challenge for teachers.

Most people have learned to maintain a surface decorum. They are too embarrassed and inhibited to say what they really think to each other, and they often do not even admit to themselves how prejudiced they are. The maintenance of such decorum and politeness is an important achievement. The attempts made on some campuses to proscribe demeaning, insensitive, and racist language operate on this level. But this is a superficial and unreliable mechanism for controlling conflict in an increasingly diverse population, and its costs to free speech rights will be unacceptable to many.

The subjects I teach, involving some of today's most controversial issues, and the way I teach, with frequent discussions of polemical writing—both tend to erode and break down the kind of reticence we depend on to get along. The idea of avoiding controversial issues altogether comes up again and again. As I have already stated, such backing away is not acceptable. These world controversies are a vital part of education. Such issues must be discussed. To omit them would be to lie to students about the world they are living in. Such discussions may also be a way to get beneath the surface, to reveal and lead students to think about more deeply held prejudices—and this is a risky process.

Recent debates about 'political correctness' and 'the canon' might seem, at first glance, to provide some guidance in meeting the dilemmas of my classroom. These debates arise out of the same problems of campus diversity and change that I face, and what is at stake in them is indeed momentous for the future of American society. How can a student body increasingly diverse in cultural background and identity be educated in our classrooms? What should such a student body be taught, especially, how should the curriculum meet and take account of the diversity of the students? What kind of society are we trying to create? How will the education we offer serve to bring about the results we want for the future of American society?

But the hotly polemical literature produced in these debates offers no guidance for dealing with real classroom situations. If we do not agree on what overall results we want and cannot measure the impact of our curricular and other academic decisions, we are certainly far from being able to arrive at any consensus about what should be happening in our classrooms. Therefore, we wrangle and accuse each other of bad faith and worse. The contributions of debaters such as Allan Bloom, Dinesh D'Souza, and Roger Kimball, or Molefi Asante, Catharine Stimpson, and Stanley Fish, tend to be stated in sweeping and absolute terms. The debate they wage, and they cannot be divided into two unified schools, is over grand strategy for the entire educational process, nationwide.

In the summary of the 'political correctness' and 'canon' debates I give here, I will state the positions in their extreme forms that critics of the positions accuse their opponents of advocating (sometimes with some justification). These summaries are composites and cannot be ascribed fully to any of the authors I have mentioned above.

Few have ever admitted to espousing 'political correctness' as such; the term has almost invariably been used ironically, even or especially by its reputed proponents. But propositions such as the following have received a good deal of support on many campuses: that an atmosphere of racism, sexism, homophobia, and intolerance pervades the campus, so that long-disadvantaged groups defined by race, gender, religion, nationality, and sexual orientation are being attacked, insulted, and excluded from the full benefits of educational and career opportunities. Rules against bigoted language and strong anti-discrimination standards, including affirmative action, are badly needed on campuses and in society generally to protect these groups.

The opponents of political correctness have seen this description of the conditions on American campuses to be exaggerated. Their description is in stark contrast, and they charge, for example, that tenured radicals in powerful positions on American campuses today have used their great power to enforce conformity to standards of political correctness on the campus community. By these standards, any deviation from correct views on race relations, abortion, gender issues, the environment, sexual orientation, or like matters is denounced and possibly even punished. In particular, a number of campuses have promulgated regulations against the use of racist language and have punished transgressors. Such regulations are a denial of free speech, and the enforcement of 'political correctness' generally has made it next to impossible to discuss some controversial issues on campus—even though it is the very purpose of colleges and universities to foster free discussion.

The closely related debate about the 'canon' is a conflict not about demeanor but about curriculum. It is in a sense about whether the diversity of American students is something to be overcome or nurtured. Conservatives want to retain at the center of the curriculum a body of literature and history they regard as key to our cultural tradition. They hold, especially, that a Canon of the best that has been thought and known, in particular the heritage of literature produced in Greece, Rome, and Europe, is an essential part of a liberal education. This Canon can be expanded to include hitherto excluded works from other cultural traditions, works by women, etc., but works included merely for their ideological message and otherwise inferior works assigned merely because they represent minority viewpoints have no place in it. Courses including such works are really political 'feel-good' courses with shoddy intellectual standards and inferior content.

The radicals or innovators want to make decisive changes in the curriculum, and they assert that the traditional Canon is a sexist and racist body of writing. It is the product of a narrow group of 'dead, white, European males,' and the claims of these writings to universality are thereby false. Greece was a slave society whose works are not exemplary. In any case, for many students of diverse cultural backgrounds, this body of writing represents someone else's cultural heritage, not their own. And to overcome past oppression and develop their own identity, many such students need to be given works from their own cultural background.

I have followed these debates carefully, but they do not solve the problems I meet in my classrooms. I agree with all of the positions; I agree with none of them. The traditionally canonical writings should be included in today's curriculum, but I would also strongly favor the inclusion of the history and literature of other cultures and regions. Then, too, the enforcement of doctrines of political correctness, where they exist, might well involve the denial of free speech, as does the freewheeling attack on academia from the right, as represented by such groups as Accuracy in Academia. In personal experience on my campus and in wide contacts on several other campuses, I have not found either to be as prevalent as the media coverage would indicate. I am worried equally about both.

Taken all in all, much of this discussion does not mean much to me. For one thing, as already noted, the strident and polemical tone of much of this writing is unproductive. What many of these writers have done is to conflate complex issues into simple ones, so that their readers outside the academy can understand who the villains are. These are serious questions, and, to me, such questions require deliberation, reflection, and a broad exchange of views. The popular debates have rather recounted many anecdotes of unreasonable positions taken. Both sides recount how the other threatens liberty, high standards, free opportunity, or the integrity of academic institutions.

What is needed, it seems to me, are not horror stories but fuller accounts of the very processes of teaching and learning, by which problems of mutual understanding and communications are met, wrestled with, possibly solved. Or even if not solved, fully aired. On many campuses, indeed, something like this is already happening. Amid all the polemics, educators are proceeding to frame new sets of core and distribution requirements, which often resemble the breadth requirements of twenty-five years ago.

In these initiatives, the concept of *pluralism* is heard over and over. The term has acquired enormous currency in the United States recently, especially in the context of higher education. Perhaps the search for pluralism in education offers a chance to transcend the strident debates now going on and channel them into more constructive, less divisive terms. To evaluate this possibility, I need first to explore the meaning of the term. Along with this new popularity, it has undergone some shift of meaning. In previous usage, pluralism had at least two distinct meanings.

In the sociology of the Third World, the term has been associated with the study of plural societies, such as Malaya, Indonesia, Fiji, Sri Lanka, Lebanon, or Cyprus, in which a territory's population is divided between two or more distinct racial, linguistic, or religious communities often—usually—in conflict with one another. The quest for political systems capable of accommodating the interests of conflicting communities and overcoming endemic conflict has been a prime factor in the twentieth century histories of all of these societies. In this sense, pluralism has been something to be overcome. The term has, on balance, a negative connotation.

A markedly contrasting usage occurs in American political science. In this tradition, the term refers to the multiplicity of competing interests in American society and their successful mediation in the political system. In *A Preface to Democratic Theory*, Robert A. Dahl described the mechanism by which the overlapping diversities cutting through society prevent a tyranny of the majority. He cites the view as popular but empirically unproven:

> If most individuals in the society identify themselves with more than one group, then there is some positive probability that any majority contains individuals who identify themselves for certain purposes with the threatened minority. Members of the threatened minority who strongly prefer their alternative will make their feelings known to these members of the tentative majority who also, at some psychological level, identify themselves with the minority. Some of these sympathizers will shift their support away from the majority alternative and the majority will crumble. (pp. 104–105)

This usage of *pluralism* is, then, distinctly positive, with the emphasis on the successful accommodation of diverse perspectives rather than the unfortunate existence of deep cleavages, which divide the very society into irreconcilable elements.

In the new American usage of the term, attention is heavily focused on ethnic and racial divisions in American society. In this way, the meaning moves toward that standard in Third World sociology, even though the actual social divisions being described are more muted, less fundamental in the United States than in, say, the Punjab or Sri Lanka, where ethnic violence has become chronic. Nevertheless, in this new American usage, pluralism retains its positive content as the name for the solution to the problem rather than the problem itself. And the venue for pluralism to act out its healing influence is education, especially higher education.

As I understand the new usage, pluralism (the variant term *multiculturalism* is also used in this context) is a particular kind of educational initiative for dealing with the problems of diversity in American society. To define this pluralist option as against others, I can now recast the debate over the direction of higher education by listing four separate ways in which the United States' educational system could deal with the problems of greater and greater cultural and linguistic diversity.

Position 1.   Unilateral, forced, hegemonic assimilation to a single norm, based on white Anglo-Saxon cultural standards.

Position 2.   Creation of a common society through the mixing of a variety of cultural tributaries, with reciprocal assimilation and no one cultural tradition in a dominating position.

Position 3.   Maintenance of a mosaic society, in which the distinct cultural patterns of various groups are studied, valued, and celebrated by individual communities and by all members of the society.

Position 4.   All out ethnic and racial separatism, with these divisions the primary badges of identity in the society and with each community concerned to defend itself against oppression from other groups.

The pluralism so much talked about in higher education today is located in the two middle positions. Debate between these positions has been noisy, and there has been a strong tendency on both sides to paint opponents as extremist enemies of freedom and justice. In the heated debates on such issues as language education, the first and fourth positions thus become accusations, fears, bogeys; few admit to advocating these positions in their extreme form, but accuse opponents of doing so. On the one hand, oppressed minorities, aggrieved by exclusion and threatened by forced assimilation, seek solidarity as their best defense. On the other hand, those whose priority is the common society see strong assertions of group identity as moves to an exclusivist separatism pushing the society toward conflict.

Despite these acrimonious squabbles, the differences between many of the debaters are mainly of nuance and emphasis, their positions often close to one another. The second position emphasizes movement toward a common society, but by a voluntary and gradual process, in which the common society forms by the mixing of the several source cultures. This position is an ideal expressed by some educators; it implies an equality between cultural traditions that does not exist in the United States. The third position emphasizes retention of the cultural traditions. It is unrealistic in its assumption that cultural practices can remain fixed despite the powerful assimilative forces in the society. In the ordinary course of social change and through the efforts of educators to teach students about diversity, the third position will really translate itself into the second. What are now very heated debates over curriculum and over more general cultural goals of education may lose their urgency quite rapidly as these nuances recede in importance.

Pluralism, in its new usage in American education, then, involves the recognition, acceptance, and celebration of cultural diversity in American life. Education for life in the pluralist society will foster knowledge and appreciation for a rich variety of culture streams which flow into American society. And, to achieve this kind of knowledge, the various cultures would be studied not only as they occur within the United States; still more important, in my opinion, is knowledge of the history, literature, and society of the various world regions which have contributed to this cultural goulash. That, at least, is where my priority is placed and where my efforts are focused.

The goals that educators on numerous campuses across the country have assigned to their faculties is an ambitious one: To head off and overcome conflict, to enable an increasingly diverse population to get along together, to right previous wrongs and achieve justice for all. All this, it seems, is to be accomplished by having our students learn about and accept our multicultural diversity.

Put in these stark terms, the pursuit of these goals seems overwhelmingly difficult. Merely putting some new courses and programs into place will not be sufficient. What courses? Who will take them? In what spirit will they be taught? This kind of educational miracle cure for our social problems seems, on the face of it, unrealistic. At least we should not expect quick results.

The quest for quick results leads to self-defeating measures. This is well illustrated by the debate over political correctness, referred to earlier, especially the attempts of some campuses to ban any and all racist, demeaning, insulting or insensitive language in student life and in teaching. Whether the tendency to enforce such standards of political correctness is as powerful and pervasive as Dinesh D'Souza and other authors have stated is open to debate. But it is clear that the phenomenon does exist, and it has always existed. This kind of self-censoring has been present on campuses for many years. Powerful interests in the society, such as religious institutions, can be sure that not many faculty will criticize them. But this kind of restraint is now being demanded on behalf of groups that were too weak in the past to claim such protection. I would regard it, wherever it exists, as a deviant, fearful, ultimately self-defeating method of dealing with intergroup prejudice and conflict.

Quite apart from their sobering First Amendment implications, such censorship projects are futile. The task of overcoming racism, which seems to be their goal, is simply much more difficult and will be exacerbated, not diminished, by crude and facile measures of censorship. The problem of racism and the means of overcoming it are the topics of all the rest of these chapters. The impulses toward censorship of racist language, sensitivity training, and other such measures stem, it seems to me, from particular assumptions about the causes and sources of conflict among our diverse campus population.

The first relates to the new and more limited meaning of pluralism now in fashion. Its focus is still on diversity, but diversity along limited dimensions and of only certain types: race and ethnicity foremost, with gender and sexual orientation assuming similar importance more recently. Each group defined by these categories, it is assumed, has a certain perspective and is, or should be, homogeneous. Some versions of multicultural education will, I fear, consist of teaching students the correct 'perspective' for their group. We need to transcend such limited and limiting approaches. Claims that homogeneous perspectives exist for entire racial or ethnic groups are simply not plausible, and defining such perspectives is not a credible way to study human society.

The old political science version of pluralism was more interesting in this regard. It assumed that the population was diverse along many dimensions, none of them correlated fully with others. Different loyalties and identities were salient at different times and to different degrees. Alliances were formed on many different bases and they tended to cancel each other out. One implication of this model is that our present obsession with these few, severely limited aspects of diversity is quite likely to be temporary.

I am not saying that racial and ethnic divisions do not exist or should not exist. I suggest, rather, that they are not natural features of society but stem from one set of priorities. A given 'perspective' is produced by a social movement, not by an ethnic group as such.

But the tendency now is to validate certain groups defined only on the basis of race, ethnicity, gender, sexual orientation, at the expense of other kinds of alignment. In the history of our society, these groups have been oppressed, and we are rightly concerned to end such oppression once and for all. But, again, there are no shortcuts.

One attempted shortcut is to single out one villain by assuming that bigotry stems from one source: the white, male, European, probably Protestant element whose language and behavior are under particular scrutiny in the enforcement of campus regulations. Dinesh D'Souza has charged that, on many campuses, the bigoted statements of white males are punishable while those of minorities are legitimized as an expression of grievance. Again, I am not sure how general this phenomenon is, but it is clear that it is self-defeating as a measure against racism. The white males—they are a category, not a group, and certainly do not share a single perspective—are not guilty to the utmost generation for past injustices. All human beings share the tendencies to fear, xenophobia, and prejudice. In a larger historical perspective, Turks, Mongols, Zulu, Brahmins, and many other peoples, not just white Europeans, have been conquerors or oppressors. I do not say this to belittle white oppression or to blame others but to make another point: even though, in our history, the abuses of power of whites over people of color were the main expression of this common human trait, even though, too, the anger of the oppressed is understandable, it still will not do to focus only on the one source and type of prejudice.

To be successful, the education in pluralism must oppose all kinds of bigotry. And the project must be based on free speech. My guiding assumption in all of these essays will be that liberty is the only basis for harmony in a pluralist society. Your liberty is the only basis for my liberty. As George M. Fredrickson has pointed out, even the liberty of the hitherto dominant group can provide a basis for the liberty of all the rest:

> . . . America's best chance for succeeding as a cohesive multicultural nation may come from a realization that the principles on which the nation was founded . . . can serve as the ideological basis for a truly democratic and multicultural America. (*New York Times Book Review*, August 22, 1993, p. 17).

Thus, neither side in the culture wars has provided a solution to the problems I face in the classroom. I am concerned both with the group-based claims for cultural expression and economic justice *and* with the preservation of individual liberty; and I want to transcend the debate as it has been carried on up to now. Given our conflicting moral orientations, religious commitments, political ideologies, and group allegiances, we simply cannot expect to arrive at consensual answers. Our answers will differ. But if we can at least ask the same questions, then a common discussion can proceed. This is not a casual statement but would involve a dramatic redefinition of what students should be learning and how they would learn it. To be in this way 'friends in our questions' might offer an answer to these dilemmas that could be sufficient for the classroom and our society. To explore whether this can be done is the central focus of this book. The strategy I will propose for achieving this goal is a collective, classroom pursuit of 'Gandhian truth,' and this approach, introduced in chapter 3, informs the entire book, providing an antidote to the positivist and relativist perspectives that many students bring with them. The chapters thus describe a certain approach to teaching this subject matter to this audience, and if they are successful they will exemplify in themselves the approach they describe.

From my perspective, my own classroom, I see the achievement of an educational pluralism as supremely difficult. I start with the daily task of reducing misunderstanding and facilitating discussion. I struggle in every class meeting to bring the diverse student audience into a single conversation, sufficiently unified and harmonious to enable all to participate and learn, while avoiding an authoritarian pedagogy that would stifle individual viewpoints. And these are, to my mind, only tentative first steps.

In any discussion of the crisis of American higher education, the commission reports and think tank surveys will no doubt get the most attention. I am increasingly convinced, though, that the experience of a single classroom can provide vital evidence for understanding these problems. The stakes are high: One payoff is the existence of a citizenry knowledgeable enough in world affairs to make democracy work in an era when foreign affairs loom large in our politics; another is the freedom to discuss and the very possibility of discussion of controversial subjects about which there exist division and sensitivity among students, on the campus, and in society generally.

Behind these rest our ability to overcome conflict, maintain harmony, open opportunities, and achieve justice in American society. The individual classrooms that once seemed so remote and unimportant are thus becoming central locations in which some of the most important issues of our society are being fought out.

NOTES

1. Reprinted from the poem "Sleepwalking," in *Climbing the Stairs*, by Mark Vinz. Spoon River Poetry Press, 1983. Used by permission of the author.

2. Reprinted from the poem beginning "So you are thinking of principles," in Josephine Miles, *Kinds of Affection*, copyright 1967 by Josephine Miles, Wesleyan University Press reprinted by permission of the University Press of New England.

3. Quoted from "Depth, Span, and Relevance," by Philip D. Curtin, from *American Historical Review*, LXXXIX (February 1984). Used by permission of the author.

2

Conflicting Views of the Classroom Revolution

Speak the word *colleagues*, as if it means
The tapestry of suffering woven with dancing
Figures of argument, knowledge suffused
Finally with communal joy's transforming power.

James Schevill, "Colleagues," *Ambiguous Dancers of Fame*.[1]

The changes that have occurred in college teaching since I entered the University of Wisconsin as a freshman in 1953 are enormous and encompass the issues now so much under debate— what should be taught in the college classroom, and how it should be taught. The history of these changes is, in a way, part of the debate. There are distinct conservative and radical versions of this history. Both have some validity, both are describing real events and patterns of change; but neither accords entirely with my own experience.

After briefly setting down key points in the conservative and radical versions, I will describe in some detail three teachers I had at Wisconsin and at the University of California at Berkeley, where I went for a master's degree in 1957. My examination of the style of these teachers, the content of their courses, and their relationship to their subject and the students will serve as a way for me to provide my own view of the classroom revolution, one different from either the conservative or radical view.

The conservatives' version of this history records and deplores the decline of higher education, setting the worst changes during the campus unrest of the Vietnam war period. They see the radical politicization of classroom and curriculum and the abandonment of objective standards of scholarship and teaching as enduring legacies of that period. In many cases, they charge, teachers no longer systematically 'covered' traditional subject matter in courses but engaged in ideological pleading. Along with these changes came grade inflation and the encouragement of students to express their feelings rather than to study and master a subject. With the prevalence of 'values relativism', such expressions were valid and could not be gainsaid.

In the 1980s, in this version, such trends resumed and intensified, as Vietnam era radicals came into positions of authority in universities. In addition, new incursions of French critical theory, such as deconstruction, and poststructuralism, were undermining the very basis of literate knowledge itself. Here we arrive back at the debate over the canon and political correctness, whose content I summarized in chapter 1.

The radical version of the history would accept some of the factual content of this conservative version but sharply reverse its values. In talking about student self-expression, for example, they would hail the end of the old authoritarian classroom, where the teacher had been the sole source of knowledge. They would plead guilty of running political classrooms but would assert that this was nothing new. Marxist and other radical scholars had long said that 'objective' teaching and writing was ideologically loaded in support of existing economic and political arrangements, in its content and emphasis and even at times in what was *not* said.

Above all, radicals would take credit for a positive and beneficial revolution in curriculum—the addition of Black Studies and the proliferation of courses in African, Asian, and Latin American history and politics during the late 1960s. Twenty years later, so-called radicals are waging a similar curricular battle, as Women's Studies, Native American and Latino, even Gay Studies claim a place in the curriculum. Again, this trend merges with the current debates about the canon and political correctness already discussed.

It is in these curricular changes that the conservative-radical debate is most clearly joined. Here, the two sides agree substantially about what is happening, but where radicals see a triumphant breakthrough, conservatives fear the dilution or even abandonment of all that is good, true, and beautiful in the traditional curriculum.

I entered the Integrated Liberal Studies (ILS) program at the University of Wisconsin in 1953, innocent of these issues. But my experience of that time is a good baseline as I work out my own version of the recent history of the American college classroom. ILS was a kind of college within a college, in which about two hundred students took their underclass requirements in science, social science, and humanities in separate courses. The program was inspired in part by Alexander Meiklejohn's Experimental College of the late 1920s and early 1930s. ILS still exists though much changed since my time.

The centerpiece of the program when I was an undergraduate was Walter R. Agard's and Paul MacKendrick's class on Greek and Roman Culture. This class was a remnant of the freshman year study of Periclean Athens in the Experimental College, in which Agard had participated.

Agard's teaching was famous, indeed legendary; he had been cited in *Life* magazine in 1950 as one of the "great teachers" of the country. His classes provide a good example of the old pre-campus-revolution classroom at its best. Agard himself, surely, represents a great deal that was valuable, and certainly in the conservative version would be valuable still, in an older educational ideal. He also represents some of the limitations of a past we cannot, in any case, go back to.

Agard's lectures were set pieces, expository, authoritative, polished. He told us all about Socrates, but he was not Socratic in his approach. He was lucid, but articulate rather than eloquent. His lectures seemed gentle yet vibrant with excitement. It was certainly his style that accounted for a good deal of his great popularity. In some years, if you missed his lecture, you could tune in later in the day to WHA, the university radio station, to listen. People all over Wisconsin would be listening, too. His class sessions more often than not ended in sustained applause. When about 1962 he offered his final course on Greek mythology it drew 1600 students.

His style was memorable, but still more important was what he was saying. 'What democracy meant to the Greeks' would provide vital lessons for the students, also living in a democracy. With Aristophanean wit, we would occasionally mutter that what democracy meant to the Greeks was that Pericles was a New Dealer. We could be irreverent but not downright disrespectful. When he started to talk, he had our rapt attention. Studying Sophocles or Thucydides, Agard argued, taught students something about human nature and about political democracy. These writings were monuments for the ages. Agard somehow put across that if you did not read Thucydides' Melian dialogue, you were not letting Agard down but letting Thucydides down—for unless you read it he had written it in vain. And not to read it was to let yourself down above all, for reading it would help you realize a greater part of your own human worth.

Agard undoubtedly idealized Greek democracy, though he also showed why it declined and eventually failed. He mentioned Athenian slavery but did not dwell on it. Since Agard did not shy away from making strong modern parallels, both the ideals of Greek democracy and its failure and decline come to my mind now. His account was the more convincing at the time because he himself, in his courtesy, humanity, and clarity seemed to represent the ideals he ascribed to the Greeks.

It is a little difficult, now, to account for Agard's great popularity. I believe it was largely the sense of closure and easy understanding that he gave to students. In his class, after going over a long, difficult reading of Aeschylus or Euripides, he made the readings so delightfully clear that it seemed a miracle.

Besides their ease and clarity, the lectures provided a full synthesis of the subject. Here was the information we thought we needed. I have the sense that it was pretty much the same information, year in and year out. Any notion, too, that this was a neutral, objective presentation is highly dubious. If anything, the ideological message was the dominant feature. With our jokes about the New Deal, even we saw that. But Agard was so loved by students, even the conservatives among them, that no one minded.

This emphasis on civic values, carried over from the Meiklejohn experiment, left an optimistic feeling that democracy was possible and right, and the decline of Athens seemed sad and unnecessary, the result of pride, ambition, and avoidable mistakes.

In the twentieth-century history of American universities, Agard is a familiar figure. At one time, most large universities had one or more such figures—the great, eloquent teachers whose courses were legendary. But the days of their authority and popularity were coming to an end. Max Savelle's course at the University of Washington had been one of these legends. The first student course evaluation at Washington in 1965 gave it the highest possible marks. But only a few years later, after his retirement but still with his characteristic youthful vigor, Savelle taught the course at a middle western university. Students, he recounted afterward, had been restless, critical, questioning, and a little hostile. The campus was changing. Savelle had run into the Vietnam era unrest and some of the changes recounted in the conservative history of university teaching.

But a closer look at Agard and his era reveal that some of the changes commonly ascribed to the upheavals of the 1960s had really occurred much earlier. The doctrine of relativism and the idea that history should be made 'relevant' to contemporary problems do not come from the French critical theory popular in the last few years; nor do they date from thirty years ago and the Vietnam era. These ideas date from at least sixty years ago:

> To establish the facts is always in order, and is indeed the first duty of the historian; but to suppose that the facts, once established in all their fullness, will 'speak for themselves' is an illusion. . . . It should be a relief to us to renounce omniscience, to recognize that every generation, our own included, will, must inevitably, understand the past and anticipate the future in the light of its own restricted experience, must inevitably play on the dead whatever tricks it finds necessary for its own peace of mind. . . . Our proper function is not to repeat the past but to make use of it, to correct and rationalize for common use. (Becker, *Everyman His Own Historian*, 249, 253)

Thus Carl L. Becker's 1931 American Historical Association Presidential Address. Its relativist argument was already present in the Greek and Roman Culture class in ILS, and indeed in many Wisconsin classrooms of the 1950s. And not only at Wisconsin. Becker's writings were standard for history graduate students all across the country in these years, and their influence on the profession was enormous. When later I first read Carl Becker's essay, I recognized the arguments immediately.

In that same time, 1932, Alexander Meiklejohn published an account of his work in the Experimental College. The reasons he gives for students to study fifth and fourth century Athens de-emphasizes their mastery of full factual information:

We should not send our students into a human situation
as tourists go to a foreign country—with a list of important
items to see and check. They should go rather as residents,
for a time, sharing, so far as they can, in the life and
experience of the people—getting the feel and the sense
of their scheme of living. In the latter case they may have
little to tell when they return, but they may perhaps be
more reasonable and intelligent in their attitudes toward
'foreign' people. (*The Experimental College*, 30)

In a way that seems ironic in the context of today's debates, the
study of ancient Greece is here justified for presentist purposes and
particularly as a means of overcoming ethnocentrism. Such issues
go back much farther than contemporary debaters normally allow.

Not all go back as far as the 1930s. I note here another set of
marked changes in classroom presentation, in how classes were
conducted, during my years as a student in the 1950s. These changes,
too, are earlier than in the conservative account and had no
connection with the political radicalism of the Vietnam war period.
In this set of changes, the set-piece expository lecture gave way to
a more informal style in which the professor made interpretive
comments on the subject. This kind of lecture was discussable
because it was a discussion. The teacher more than almost any other
who showed me this way was Robert J. Brentano, whose class on
medieval British history I took at Berkeley. In 1957 and 1958 when
I had his course, he was just starting out and was barely over thirty
years old.

The contrast with the veteran Agard could not have been greater.
Brentano thought out loud, and one had the feeling that neither
he nor anyone else had ever said these things before. It was new,
and we were in on it. Coming in (on one occasion) a few minutes
late for class —"Sorry, but a new Kingsley Amis novel has just
arrived," he said—he would start to talk. "You know what I mean,"
he might say, at precisely the moment when we did not. But just
after this moment of confusion could be an epiphany. Glossing a
document, we could suddenly see more deeply and more clearly
the different levels of meaning and interpretation that were possible.

Besides the ceaseless exercises in interpretation in class, Brentano
revealed to me a new and radical vision of historical significance.
What were the objects that Ailred of Rievaulx wanted to have around

him as he lay dying? No, not quite that, but what did those objects mean, what was Ailred thinking? Again, what was the circular shape of Anselm's thought? Or how could we account for the change from foursquare, stiff crucifixes to emotional ones, depicting a suffering Christ? We dwelt on these things at length. I remember spending twelve weeks on the period from 1066 to 1300, leaving only two or three for the fourteenth and fifteenth centuries. "But nothing different happened then," he said.

Some conservative critics have strongly attacked this style of teaching and lamented the decline of the old fact-based, chronological history. Often, they blame political radicals, who have infiltrated academe with their private, ideological agendas. They are wrong. Brentano, a devout Catholic, was (is) deeply immersed in medieval history and its interpretation. But the familiar stories through which a standard body of information about medieval history had been presented no longer seemed sufficient. There were other sources to consider, other questions to ask, more to be known. Brentano did not believe that history should be easy or pretty. In his essay in *The Historian's Workshop*, he defined the kind of history he wanted to write:

> I think, and thought, that history should be allowed to be, should be made to be, as demanding (and always as complex) as a play or a novel. . . . Why should people who are willing in patience to listen through a play like *Waiting for Godot* in the hope that they will have some little understanding of it, some experience from it, turn to history and demand the slick prettiness and intelligibility of Trevelyan or, at the other extreme, the statistical, sociological firmness of clear answers in matters in which they must know there are no real answers. . . . If history is worth writing at all, it must be written 'real,' with the violent and complex reality of serious fiction. (pp. 25–26)

This sense that historical interpretation was difficult and open-ended came over in Brentano's teaching. His style put greater demands on students and brought them more deeply into the subject of study. In invoking fiction and drama, Brentano did not mean that he would write fiction; he was fully committed to maintaining the factual integrity of his teaching and writing. He meant that history should be, was, demanding. Students should be willing to engage in tough intellectual work. Agard's teaching, like G. M. Trevelyan's writing of British history, he would have judged as too polished and easy, with all problems apparently solved, all judgments final.

The change of style that conservative critics lament from objective history to radical ideological pleading is not the change that I witnessed; the real change is rather from an easy, definitive story serving a clear civic purpose, over to a deeply committed quest for understanding of any historical period, in which the implications are varied and unpredictable. It may at times be the unpredictability that conservatives dislike.

When later back at Wisconsin I came to take written examinations on British history, I was glad I had read G. O. Sayles on the Angevin Empire and the origins of Parliament; the old views of significance still very much governed British history there. But thirty years later, it is the attempt to think along with Ailred or Anselm that I remember best and that has most influenced the way I would like to teach. In this style of teaching, in which classes were original, discursive, probing, with tentative and flexible conclusions, I saw real possibilities. Here was something I could do. Brentano therefore became much more of a role model to me than Agard, whose style I could not have imitated anyway.

The curricular revolution, the revolution in what is taught in the classroom, also began somewhat earlier and under different auspices than either conservative or radical combatants usually state. Just about the time I was moving from undergraduate to graduate school in 1957, whole new fields were transforming the history and social sciences curriculum. South and Southeast Asian, Chinese, African, Islamic, Latin American, and Pacific histories and cultures all came into their own at the larger universities. In the name of national defense, the federal government provided money for the study of nonwestern languages to graduate students (at least those willing to swear their loyalty), and foundations provided fellowships for research. A whole new generation of faculty trained in these new disciplines went to new jobs all over the country. The impetus came in significant part from Cold War priorities, but this factor had more to do with institutional support and did not always govern the scholarship and teaching of these subjects. In any case, the programs and library collections that radicals would later demand were already in place at many schools as a result of these initiatives.

Here was my career choice, and the teacher who led me to this choice was Philip D. Curtin. Curtin came to the University of Wisconsin from Swarthmore in 1956. He too was near the beginning of his career, a young assistant professor, his books on African history, his receiving of the MacArthur Fellowship, the Presidency of the American Historical Association, all in the future.

Curtin's early career at Wisconsin, when he developed the programs in African history and 'Comparative Tropical History,' (later Comparative World History), coincided with my doctoral work under his direction. Here was a revolution in historiography and education but, again, not the revolution that conservatives and radicals have described.

The late 1950s and early 1960s were the years of decolonization in Africa, and I point out in chapter 11 how the development of African history is connected with those events, giving African history a persistent presentist quality. Working under Curtin, this was less obvious. Curtin was not a Cold War scholar, still less a fire engine chaser looking to take up the latest hot topics.

Curtin's training at Harvard had been in European history, but within this field he emphasized Europe's relations with other societies. Thus when he went on the job market, it was not as an Africanist but as a British Empire historian, and his first books, *Two Jamaicas* and *The Image of Africa,* can be seen as developments of that older field. By overcoming the limitations of the older approach, however, they really helped create new fields. The first book, about 'the role of ideas in a tropical colony', exhibited a broader new intellectual history in which the ruled as well as the rulers, the broader public as well as the literary elite, were included. The second, a study of 'British ideas and action', was again an intellectual history. The themes were the development of British information (and misinformation) about Africa, doctrines of racism, and rationales for imperialist intervention. The approach was, in a sense, still British Empire history, but the account was fully informed from the African side to an extent no previous work had achieved.

The governing necessity of teaching, research, and writing for Curtin was *span*, a term earlier used by W. K. Hancock. In Hancock's description,

Span reveals itself in historical or sociological work as an awareness of background; it places the object of immediate and intense study in its proper perspective with the other objects, near or distant, to which it is necessarily related. (*Survey of British Commonwealth Affairs*, II, Part 2, 331)

The breadth of knowledge needed to explain even a small historical problem was simply greater than the traditional fields of study, and training in those fields, had enabled historians to cope with.

This quality of far reaching inquiry runs through Curtin's work and the training he offered to students. A paper I heard him give at the American Historical Association in the early 1970s provides a good example. It was called "The Lure of Bambuk Gold." Like many of his class lectures, the paper looked at a topic from a wide variety of angles. Discussing Bambuk gold, Curtin went easily and confidently from quantitative analysis, to geology and mining technology, to European monetary theory, to historical and anthropological treatments of West African peoples. It was a dazzling display of the 'span' he wanted us all to develop. All this with a rapid fire but clear and lucid flow of argument and example, and yet he was summarizing a longer paper and remaining within the alloted time. I have never heard anyone do it better.

In seminars, we struggled to get even a fraction of this clarity and force. We learned that doing it over and over again, getting on top of the material, was the way anyone—including Curtin himself— had to proceed. "Easy reading comes from hard writing," he said. At seminar meetings each week we criticized each other's papers in every possible respect, from grammar and punctuation to arguments about research techniques and the interpretation of evidence.

Curtin's next books, *The Image of Africa*, *The Atlantic Slave Trade*, and *Africa Remembered* were contributions to African history, even though an awareness of European imperial history was part of the 'span' that supported them. The seminar, too, increasingly focused on Africa.

The case Curtin and other historians of Africa were making was that Africa had a history—that African experience could be studied and understood historically, that this history was recoverable and significant. As a corrective to past practices, they called for the study of the subject 'from the inside', emphasizing the African voice and African sources. Though some went overboard in this direction, the commitment to an African history in Curtin's work never spelled the omission of European elements but rather a determination to look at a given problem from any angle needed to provide an adequate explanation.

Curtin and his fellow Africanists won the battle for the status and significance of African history by about 1970. By then, more and more history departments were hiring Africanists, not a few of them graduates of the Wisconsin program, as skeptical departments were won over by the quality of the research being done. That was the revolution that brought African history to American universities.

The nationwide struggle for Black Studies departments was waged separately, beginning a little later, for distinctly different purposes. Despite the rhetoric about getting African American and African history and culture taught 'for the first time', the real innovation was the hiring of black faculty, recruiting of black students, and establishment of a program to orient these students to college life. In many cases, especially in the early years, this meant emphasizing the ideological messages of 'the Movement'. One common outcome was the creation of single-audience courses and the kind of 'insiderism' I discuss in chapter 4. I must add that many programs transcended these limitations as they matured.

Yet such problems are not overcome entirely. The recent struggle of Afrocentrists to place African material in the curriculum, seemingly repeating the old battle for the status and validity of African studies, is often something very different—an even more emphatic insistence on a certain African American cultural-political agenda in the curriculum. The earlier victory for African history, *and* the original struggle for Black Studies programs, were waged on markedly more advantageous ground than that now being staked out in the Afrocentrist movement.

This account of the teaching of Agard, Brentano, and Curtin is my answer to the conservative and radical histories of recent higher education. It is, I am aware, a personal and idiosyncratic account. Colleagues who were at Berkeley and Wisconsin in the same period have markedly different perceptions. And though neither the conservative nor the radical versions accord with my experience, they are dominant. The conflict between them is widespread, and this conflict pervades the environment in which I have to teach.

I choose to occupy a middle ground, accepting parts of both positions and finding something to fear from both sides. I am not here following the path of a wishywashy, liberal trimmer. Attacks threatening the freedom to teach could come from either side, and the colleaguiality on which the best higher education depends is in some places threatened.

It is, in short, a dangerous time to be a teacher of certain subjects in an American university. This book is my answer to these actual and potential attacks, my defense against the dangers higher education faces.

NOTE

1. Reprinted from the poem, "Colleagues," in *Ambiguous Dancers of Fame* by James Schevill. © James Schevill 1987. Swallow Press/Ohio University Press, 1987. Used by permission of the publisher.

3

The Teacher's Pitch and the Student Audience

If you complete this program, you will have friends
From all the rich races of your human blood:
Meanwhile, engage in the often friendless struggle.
A long war, a pygmy war in ways,
But island by island we must go across.

William Meredith, "Do Not Embrace Your Mind's New Negro Friend"
Partial Accounts.[1]

When I am teaching a course, I am never satisfied with how it is going. I may have covered the appropriate subject matter, but I am nagged by doubts. Have I put over that intangible element I want the students to retain when they have forgotten the factual details? When I examine more closely what I think is missing, I believe that several presuppositions behind my teaching are never systematically stated. Perhaps they are not explicit enough in my own mind, so that I fail to make them clear to the classes I teach. I want here to spell them out.

I am aware that it is I, not the students, who are most dissatisfied. They and I have different expectations, which I realize when I say something particularly apposite and see them all looking at me, while when I repeat a set of routine and humdrum facts from the textbook, their heads go down to write. This information is often what students want. They expect to receive from their attendance a set of definitive lecture notes that they can possess, review, and that will allow them to 'acquire' and 'have' the subject. The more I fulfill these expectations, the worse I feel about my teaching. The routine and systematic survey of a subject that many students might well like, is both too easy and too much trouble. I do not do it, either because it is not what I think I should be doing or because I am too lazy to work it all out.

This feeling goes way back to the beginning of my teaching career. In my first year of teaching, in the University of Washington history department in 1963, fresh from graduate school in Madison, I worked long hours preparing the lecture for each class. "It is a tough year," said a concerned and sympathetic senior colleague. "Yes," I replied. "It is a tough year," he repeated, "But then *you will be done!*"

But at the end of the year I was not done. I am still not 'done' more than twenty-five years later. I never did create that set of finished set-piece lecture notes that I could take up and deliver in order at the appropriate point in each of my courses. Down to today, each time I enter the classroom, I feel a little of the same panic and ignorance as I begin, Brentano-like, to think out loud in front of the students.

Some, not all, of the students would be more pleased with me if I had indeed gotten 'done'. Some would not, and I would not. But I do need to be careful to explain what I am doing, for I am not trying and failing to present set-pieces to 'cover' the subject. The very arrangement of the room, with the teacher standing in front and lecturing, contributes to the misunderstanding by giving me authority. The students, pens poised, accept my authority. They do not want their fellow students to talk too much—what do they know? But I hope they will talk; I might learn something.

What the students get from me, at this point, is a commentary on the subject at hand. One of the major reasons I do not use set-piece lectures, prepared for all time, is that even if no one else talks, my lecture should be a discussion with the particular audience I am facing. The statements I, or any lecturer, make, are not, cannot be, fixed, positivist renditions of reality. Their impact is decisively shaped by the listening audience, and I need to know a great deal about that audience in order to teach effectively. I would suggest that few university teachers know nearly enough about their students, and that that is a major weakness in their teaching. Knowing and responding to the audience more effectively may be that intangible which would make me more satisfied with my courses. And if students had this explanation of how I was operating, the benefit might be doubled.

Alas, students do not understand me—it is such an easy and escapist reaction. Is it their fault or mine? Over years I hope I have learned that it is no one's fault, but that it is impossible to make neutral, objective statements whose meaning is manifestly clear and identical for all listeners. Anything I say in the classroom will be taken in unexpected ways. That is why discussion and feedback are necessary, and testing the effectiveness of communication is certainly one of the major purposes of examinations.

The teacher had better know the audience. It is more than finding out what background information students possess or lack. Their entire mindset, experience, biases, presuppositions, unexamined assumptions influence the way the teacher's statements will be taken.

Over years of teaching courses on African history, European expansion and imperialism, and colonial and imperial history, I have gradually identified certain persistent student preconceptions that recur year in and year out. I do not claim that all students are alike in these ways; the ideological, experiential, and social diversity of the audience is very great indeed. But the same themes come up over and over again in student reactions to what I am saying.

The pitch of my teaching is tilted subtly against the various biases I have identified, with a goal not of converting students to my views but of making them aware of their own. An unexpected angle of vision from the teacher will, I hope, get their attention and make them test their assumptions. Furthermore, the steady pitch I maintain against my audience's preconceptions is, for me, a method of attaching my statements to something, so that they are not floating loose, to be blown in a different direction by every student bias. The most common question I receive starts out with, "Are you saying that . . . ?" Usually, I am not, at least not in those simple terms. "Yes, but wait," I need to say.

Here, let us have some specifics about this consistent, longterm mindset I have found in the student audience I teach. As I have stated, students want information. They want closure, so that some things are settled for good and all. Many seem to be positivistic, in that they believe in a scientific language capable of rendering accurate descriptions of reality, and they believe in the prime importance of factual information objectively presented. Contradictory as it may seem, they are also relativists, their relativism coexisting with many incompatible viewpoints.

In courses on colonial and imperial history, this translates into a sympathy with cultural nationalism as students seem to believe that people, especially in the Third World, have sacrosanct cultures that they must wish to keep intact. And students believe that the world is divided in a simple and unambiguous way between imperialist oppressors and their victims—the colonizer and the colonized. Also, related to this, and this is a most difficult and tenuous generalization, they assume violence as a norm in the entire relationship of colonizer and colonized.

I am not saying that these assumptions are all mistaken, or entirely mistaken. Many of these biases put them on the side of humanity; it is good to be against imperialism. But the way students fail to think historically, falling instead into chronological foreshortening and hindsight bias, leads them to misinterpret the evidence they are confronting. These student presuppositions are a filter through which any statements I maked are passed, or a mold used to reshape my lecture material as it passes into their notes.

When I start to teach, the dominant feature of the students' mindset for me to confront is their relativism. It may seem surprising that I single out relativism as an overriding student assumption, against which I would pitch my teaching. Why not ethnocentrism? It is indeed important to combat ethnocentrism. But teaching relativism will not accomplish that. Students seem to be coated with a consistent veneer of relativism. What lies underneath?

The relativism I am talking about here is the classic 'cultural relativism' of beginning anthropology courses. It may be outdated in scholarship, but it is clearly still being taught somewhere. Over years, much of my student audience clings to it strongly.

Relativism now exists in a variety of guises and in much more sophisticated forms, but what I encounter in my student audience is quite simple. The 'other culture' is described in the 'anthropological present' as a more or less stable system. Its various components, no matter how strange, outrageous, or even immoral particular usages and customs may seem to us, are judged to be 'valid' and 'authentic' in terms of that culture. And, in functionalist analyses, these customs 'work' in the culture. Tampering with them would run the risk of throwing the entire stable system out of balance.

To condemn the customs or even criticize them too harshly, from the point of view of our own customs, would be cultural arrogance and ethnocentrism. This relativist posture seems humbly to accept the other culture as a given. But this is a mock humility, and the position can lead to a kind of arrogance, in which the relativist observer presumes to know what is valid and authentic and becomes thereby suspicious of cultural change and innovation, even if members of the society in question are the innovators.

The relativist stance disqualifies the outsider from commenting on the culture except in terms of acceptance. Often the main point of anthropological descriptions of the 'other culture' has been to learn relativism, not to learn about real people of other societies.

I realize that I am going against the common practice here. 'Other cultures' have routinely been taught for a long time through a relativist critique of ethnocentric prejudice. But what are the drawbacks of this approach to cause me to abandon it? The strategy implies, first of all, a claim that the teacher is free of the vice and that his or her teaching will cleanse the tainted students with a bath of truth. If this 'truth' is accurate information about other cultures, then that is valuable in itself, but such information does not necessarily make the audience more tolerant. In any case, this direct teacher-laying-it-on approach may be ineffective against the most bigoted element because they are bigoted and ineffective against the more subtly prejudiced, including those who assume a relativist posture, because they think the message does not apply to them.

The assumption that the teacher is free of ethnocentrism seems dangerous to make even for the most determined advocates of intercultural understanding. All human beings, living in a culture and practicing it, must make constant value choices; they are vehicles of culture, and at some level they 'believe' in what they are doing and not doing. These beliefs influence their evaluation of the entire world. It is only a matter of degree, really, between this commitment to a culture and grossly prejudiced ethnocentrism. I may be tolerant and do not think of making members of another culture follow my ways or desist from their customs; I might not even find their customs strange—for them; but inevitably I am going to see their customs from the point of view of one who lives in the context of my culture, not theirs.

What does this say about my perceptions? When I make statements or judgments of value about the other culture, my statements are distorted by my own cultural baggage, by the very language I am using. With all the good will in the world, I will be ethnocentric at some level. Where is the line between 'stereotypes,' presumably hostile, and 'generalizations,' presumably made as conscientiously as possible? The differences lie not simply in the hostility, nor in the mental process itself—stereotyping is generalization. I think the difference might lie in an awareness of what is going on mentally when I make a generalization. I must have the mental process of generalization under control, keeping my thinking tentative, remembering that my generalization is not a 'fact'.

For these reasons, a general relativist attack on the students' ethnocentrism will be ineffective. And what is worse, it will make them relativists!

An effective approach must come to terms with the real difficulties of understanding and interpreting other cultures. My assumption will be that for everyone trying to understand another culture, teacher and students alike, there is a tangle of almost insoluble puzzles and traps.

My pitch against relativism is my way of getting to some of these deeper levels. My major objections to relativism are these:

1. Students and teachers can really only pretend to shed their own cultural biases but cannot in fact do so. It seems more honest to examine our cultural starting point instead of pretending we do not have one.

2. Relativism tends to become a position students assume when the 'other cultures' question comes up. It is held in a logic-tight compartment along with many incompatible beliefs in other areas.

3. A pedagogy leaning on relativism tends to choose a description of apparently static and sometimes bizarre cultural forms, giving a quaint museum-piece picture of other societies.

4. Relativism can sometimes lead to the idealization of non-western societies, so that injustice and cruelty are interpreted as 'functional' and valid in that cultural context. To do this, inevitably, a good many things about the history of the society have to be dismissed or ignored.

5. Relativism leads to a false impression that the human race is divided into 'cultures' seen as discrete and separate entities.

6. The relativist pitch, I suspect, does not really rid students of ethnocentrism but is in fact a way of 'solving' the question of cultural difference, dismissing other cultures and not taking them truly seriously.

Of course, I do want to overcome crude expressions of ethnocentrism, but I am concerned about examining much more deeply held attitudes. And in making my pitch against relativism, how can I avoid being taken as a cultural neo-bigot?

I need to sidestep the simplistic ethnocentrism-relativism dichotomy. I am trying to explain to students something about the realities of other cultures and about a whole set of complex relationships as they occurred in the process of European expansion around the world. I start with the realization that no statement I make can ever be more than a small part of the truth, that however much complexity I try to incorporate, my major impact is one of simplification.

In place of relativism I propose Gandhian truth. Gandhi's technique was called *satyagraha*, a grasping after the truth. It is best known as a form of political action, but it can be used in the classroom in a different sense. Absolute Truth does exist, according to Gandhi; but it is not accessible to human beings. God is Truth, or, as he preferred, Truth is God. However much human beings strove, they could only achieve a partial, lower-case, provisional truth. That partial truth was the concern of Gandhi's entire career. At one and the same time, he was willing to die for his current conception of the truth and yet keep his conception tentative, ever willing to revise it if an opponent could convince him of some new element of truth. He was willing to die, but never willing to kill for his cause, because he was never on sure enough ground to justify violence.

Convinced and also tentative—a difficult combination and one we need to consider seriously; it has the uncomfortable implication that we can never reach closure, we are never on sure enough ground that we can relax our quest for a more complete truth. One implication is that it is always appropriate to listen carefully to an opposing viewpoint and even to seek common ground with it.

Students, I fear, often invest their teachers with the power to dispense Truth and feel dissatisfied that they are only getting partial bits of truth. Not only that, but in order to convey my sense of the complex reality, I have to give out many partial bits, no one of them complete in itself. When students ask, "Are you saying . . . ?" my answer is inevitably, yes, but I am saying something else too. Just wait.

What have I gained? What, in other words, is the difference between relativism and 'Gandhian truth'? In a set of analyses of the 'other culture' based on Gandhian truth, the above relativist functionalist approaches would be demoted to the status of tentative and partial viewpoints, for whatever insights they might facilitate—to be followed by other views to illuminate other aspects of the reality under study. Furthermore, the way is left open for students to make critical, even biased judgments, trying them out in discussion against individuals with differing perspectives.

Thus, I argue, the student who gives up relativism to pursue Gandhian truth is liberated in a variety of ways. Relativism is a fixed and final way of judging certain matters; Gandhian truth is an open-ended process, never finished. The relativist separates herself from the culture she is studying; the Gandhian engages that culture. The relativist must accept everything about the other culture; the Gandhian is free to make judgments.

In several ways, the relativist assumes a static position while the Gandhian is developing and changing. The relativist student of others' *mores* need not engage his own convictions; for the Gandhian, the process of refining her own beliefs is a major component of study. The relativist denies his ethnocentrism by wishing it away; the Gandhian discovers, confronts, and struggles with her own ethnocentric attitudes. The relativist is forced to divide truth into compartments, one set of valid propositions for any given society of others, another for himself. The Gandhian uses universal standards of judgment, but these are provisional and ever open to revision. The Gandhian may take a position and argue it with determination but is never fixedly sure enough of anything to leave off listening seriously to other positions. The Gandhian ever wants to progress to a sounder, better supported view of the human world. The relativist understands; the Gandhian is trying to understand and hopes that someday she might make some small gains.

Gandhian truth beckons the student to become entangled in the issues of the other culture; she is entitled to debate those issues, to be influenced by them, to take sides. Gandhi was thus engaged— he was Muslim, Hindu, Christian, Jew (though he knew much less about Judaism.) Relativism keeps the outsider as outsider, frozen out, unable to enter in. The only task of the relativist outsider is to be tolerant and avoid ethnocentrism; but otherwise, the 'other culture' does not affect him.

Gandhi the man had serious failings and serious failures. And the very field of intergroup relations is one area for which his efforts did not always turn out very well and have been severely criticized—not least by himself. He was not a systematic thinker. His actions could be arrogant and insensitive. I do not, in short, wish to idealize Gandhi. But I would argue that his humanness and his very willingness to make unceasing attempts at reconciliation and understanding are, despite his failures, exemplary. As Joan Bondurant points out, he provides a serious approach to conflict resolution and an inspiring dedication to pursue 'experiments with truth.'

In these ways, I find Gandhi's perspective useful. I am not proposing to model my classroom in any literal way on Gandhi's personal practices, and I intend no commitment to Gandhian conclusions about anything. Nor does this kind of application of Gandhi's ideas imply any particular theological commitment, as Gandhi himself noted. I have merely extrapolated from his ideas about how to seek truth. My suggestion is that they are applicable not only to political struggles for justice but also to classroom and academic inquiry, a sphere whose nonviolence seems tested in today's conflicted and confrontational atmosphere. They provide a standpoint from which an individual can enter into a kind of personally engaged dialogue with the ideas and beliefs of another culture as well as a framework for argument, for learning even while disagreeing.

Gandhian truth also challenges students' positivism. I believe the rigorous, scientifically achieved certainty they often expect is beyond our reach. The humility implied in Gandhi's idea that human beings can only achieve a partial, provisional truth seems the more vital, in that human affairs are vastly complex, and none of us, really, knows very much about them.

Reducing a complex reality in the world to a linear, verbal description resembles, in many ways, the cartographer's task of drafting a flat map of a spherical surface, the globe. To achieve one kind of accuracy, a map projection must sacrifice others. No one of the many possible map projections is more accurate than another. They are all accurate if the projection is based on mathematically consistent principles and the map is carefully drafted from reliable data. Different projections are simply suitable for different purposes; their choice depends on the kind of relationship cartographers wish to illustrate.

The world may well be so complex that, practically speaking, all is mishmash and no valid generalizations can be made about anything. But the mishmash view of the world is not interesting, or it is perhaps too upsetting. Simply to give up by saying that we cannot know or understand anything is to say that we are helpless. Nor is it acceptable to seek a more and more detailed and complex model until we approximate the complexity of the world. We must simplify to understand, and distortion is the price. These simplifications are like map projections, or, in my other image, like partial Gandhian installments of truth, whose validity depends on continued testing.

In teaching and writing, historians, like cartographers, are representing the complex world on flat pieces of paper, with the use of symbols. The world context is envelopmental and developmental, while our presentation is selective, linear, and sequencial. We cannot say everything at once, and it is hard to narrate development and describe the envelopment (context) at the same time. This is a McLuhanesque problem, but I do not recommend a McLuhanesque solution, which I imagine might be a kind of classroom 'happening' with several things going on at once. Rather, we have continually to remind the audience how our form of presentation, like a map projection, distorts reality. The reduction in scale—simplification and selection—means that we have to leave a lot out so that what we do include will be visible and coherent.

To build up a satisfying picture of the reality we are studying, we may need to pass over the same material several times. More than one approach is called for, because each one reveals only a partial picture and distorts some relationships. No one approach will accomplish everything. But if an approach succeeds in organizing some of the data effectively, then it is worthwhile. Model, formulation, intellectual construct, principle of selection, explanatory hypothesis, or whatever you call these various approaches—all distort and omit essential elements—but some of them reveal unrealized relationships by putting material into new contexts. The approaches must be wisely chosen: it is quite feasible to organize selected mishmash into nonsense, boredom, chaos, garbage, or simple lies.

The criticism of any one intellectual construct can take two forms. One is an analysis of its distortions, the things it fails to do or does badly, and this line of criticism the teacher using the approach should already have done. Gandhi would always undertake just such a self examination before he began any of his campaigns. A critic could also attempt to show that a given model or approach is not effective in illuminating the facet of reality that the user is trying to present and that another approach would work better. But again, merely to point out the elements of omission and distortion is not in itself a telling criticism. These are part of all presentations.

This long discourse comparing map projections to selective presentations of historical reality may seem to have taken us a long way from the problems of student expectations and presuppositions and from the problems of relativism and ethnocentrism.

We can now return to the issue at hand. I believe that to present a series of partial, incomplete perspectives provides a way for me as a teacher to sidestep the relativism-ethnocentrism dilemma and to set a pitch against the perceived biases of students, without simply attempting to impose my views on them. Their views and mine are two partial, Gandhian truths.

I need to tell students this as clearly as possible. As it now stands, students are eager to take what I say about anything as a final, settled account of the matter at hand, suitable to be inscribed in their notes for later use. Their priority is positive information, and they want closure; my priority is inquiry, and my procedures are open-ended.

In several later chapters, I will take up some of the subjects I teach, especially colonial and South African history, and show how some of these approaches to teaching might work in practice. These are subjects in which the student preconceptions I have described above come into play with great frequency as obstacles to clear communication. I need to find ways not to refute these biases but to get past them to deeper levels of understanding.

Each of these presentations will be a combination of truth, accompanied by omission and distortion. Each will open up an intellectual process of understanding that is never finished. Students' expectations of synthesis, of closure, and of that complete set of notes are all denied. Their own assumptions, preconceptions, and ways of thinking, I hope, are challenged but not destructively attacked. The purpose of pitching the argument against the audience is not to destroy their views but to help students become aware of them. More valuable than any particular body of information about imperial history or any other topic, might be a habit of intellectual tentativeness and self-criticism that I hope to instill as an alternative to the more frequently encountered affectation of relativism that has been so fashionable in recent decades.

I believe that intolerance, suspicion of outsiders and dislike of what is different are deep-seated tendencies for all people and all societies. The pose of relativism is a glib and emotionally inexpensive way to dismiss the problem. For our society, the consequences of intolerance are serious. If students know that overcoming it in our communities and ourselves is a long, slow process and not a matter of adopting one intellectual pose, then at least they will have a way of starting.

NOTE

1. Reprinted from the poem, "Do Not Embrace Your Mind's New Negro Friend," in the book *Partial Accounts*, by William Meredith. © William Meredith 1987. Alfred A. Knopf, 1987. Used by permission of the publisher.

4

Insiders and Outsiders

. . .
And the pain, the pain, the pain
of knowing that the pain is
eternal, that the sky shall lift up
and rain them down
and blind their eyes.

Henry Dumas, "Pane of Vision," *Knees of a Natural Man.*[1]

This chapter is an examination of ethnic background and temperament and their implications for me as a teacher. In other chapters, I look at the the interplay of controversial subjects and the diverse student audience. But the identity and personality of any given teacher is, inevitably, part of the situation.

The kind of self-assessment I am presenting here, even more than in the rest of the book, may seem a highly personal and idiosyncratic statement. I use the first person singular throughout. On one level, true, the book is personal, as my own meditation about the problems of diversity in American higher education today. But I hope this personal tone will not preclude a more general resonance, in which my personal experience can stand as an example of what everyone else also experiences, and of the problems that teachers of many different subjects, from many different backgrounds, must also face just as I do.

I am white and male. My roots go deeply back into protestant New England. This is not a fashionable background to have, and I know people who try to hide it. People of my ancestry were at one time a primary source of the nation's teachers. Indeed, they were the standard bearers of Americanism to generations of immigrants, and their task was to purvey their dominant culture to the newcomers. This made them gatekeepers, if not cultural imperialists, whose way of life was the standard of cultural value for the entire society.

All this is fortunately past. In the course of twentieth-century social change, this Anglo-Saxon dominance has ended and the group is even in some ways marginalized. My background is sometimes described as experientially deprived and disqualifying compared to an eastern, urban, working class, ethnic experience. Immigrants, including recent immigrants, Native Americans, African Americans all take a full place alongside the seventeenth-century Puritans in the richer new versions of American history, just as a broader version of World History supplants the old Western Civilization course.

When I stand before a class of students, they see in front of them a white male. Some of them may believe that white maleness will fully govern the status of whatever I say. When I am speaking about another community, they may wonder why they should listen to me instead of a member of that community. How can I answer this? I cannot be someone else, nor can I say with nineteenth-century scientific historians that it is not I speaking, but History. Carl L. Becker long ago exploded that as a pretense.

In some quarters, indeed, I am triply disqualified from understanding—by gender, ethnicity, and class—and they may suspect me of playing the old role of WASP cultural imperialist. They sometimes wonder whether I am qualified or even entitled to speak about the affairs of other nations, other confessions, the ethnics, the oppressed, the faithful of the world.

Because I must meet such attacks (if for no other reason,) my personal experience provides the basis for a more general discussion. Whatever the previous dominance of people of my ancestry and cultural heritage, in today's conditions I must be able to move beyond such particularities, just as others must do, in order to be effective in teaching a diverse student body. The colleagues with whom I have discussed these issues may be Indians, Africans, Germans, Irish, or Iranians from overseas, or Jews, Catholics, African Americans, Italian Americans, and other immigrant groups from different parts of the United States. Many of these colleagues have undergone difficult transitions from their own homogeneous ethnic upbringings to the heterogeneous, secular mix of the wider society. They speak of the same problems I face—how does their particular background affect the status of what they say or write professionally? In teaching before general and variegated audiences, then, we all have analogous problems of how to come to terms with our particular ethnic or cultural backgrounds. Any given heritage can be a source of insights in our analyses of history and society; it can also give us blind spots. The case I want to make, then, is that we are all in this together, and that the discussion I provide will raise echoes in the experiences of my colleagues.

We are all ethnics, we are all carriers of a cultural heritage. Just now ethnicity is receiving enormous emphasis. One aspect of this emphasis is the doctrine I will call *insiderism*. This rests on the idea that in certain subject areas, the ethnic identity of the teacher *ought* to govern his or her statements. The insider, the member of a racial, ethnic, or religious community is the only one worth listening to, the only one capable of making valid statements about a given cultural heritage.

Here is a direct and formidable obstacle to the education in pluralism, and I cannot accept it. In my view, it is incompatible with free academic study and teaching.

One difficulty of insiderism in practice is worth noting here: There are sharp disagreements about who is the true insider, about who can speak for the_____community. Looked at from the outside, these debates are the conflicts of authenticity which I discuss in chapter 12.

In place of these insider claims, I propose, by contrast, to assume the position of an outsider and to recommend this role to others. It provides me with a good location from which to view and analyze a variety of historical and social situations and discuss them with the multicultured student audience. In what follows, then, I will define this outsider position and argue its case against insider claims.

First, I must meet the claim, referred to above, that only insiders can understand their own affairs, the claim of 'biological insiderism' now so fashionable. In recent years, members of some communities have come close to the assertion that only 'they' can make valid statements about their community, indeed that only 'they' are even entitled to discuss their affairs.

Against this, I do not view my outsider location as a disqualification stemming from my experientially deprived background. In a sense, I regard it as an advantage, compensating in some ways for the disadvantages of not being a member of any of the ethnic, religious, or minority groups I may be discussing. And my status as an outsider does not stem from my particular background but can be communicated to others. Insiders can benefit from an outside view too, without giving up their special advantage as insiders.

Being an outsider is my profession, my inclination, my identity. Insiders recognize me immmediately as an outsider. To them, an outsider is one who does not understand the insiders' thoughts, feelings, or realities. To them, to be an insider is precisely to understand those things. Yet my very self-imposed task as an outsider is to seek understanding. Thus, outsiders and insiders are at cross purposes from the very start of the discussion. My task here is to show how this gap can be bridged.

The outsider is an academic, a person who wishes to analyze, compare, or study the human world. But if the outsider wants to understand, the insider already understands. Insiders are members of particular sacred nations, true religions, or oppressed groups. The activities they pursue in common are to celebrate their identity, to worship in the true faith, or to feel the unique emotions of their group, feelings no outsider can ever share.

The outsider takes it upon himself to compare nations, classify religions, anatomize the relations of oppressors and oppressed. To him, the uniqueness of a nation or the truth of a religion is beside the point. Nations or religions can be studied through the application of categories or criteria commond to all. In a similar manner, the experiences of oppressed groups can be rendered in patterned interpretations.

But to the insider, such outsider interpretations are at best superficial, at worst crude distortions of the particular truth or identity or experience the insider may hold. "It may be all right in general," says an insider, "But it distorts our experience." "You make an intellectual game out of our suffering," says another. "It is insulting to compare our experience to another. It is not comparable," says a third. The very things that matter most, the uniqueness, the truth, the feeling of belonging to a certain group or shared experience, are exactly what is missing from the outsiders' analyses.

In these ways and more, the outsider's attempts to speak about other groups are beset by criticisms. The outsider, the adherent of a particular nationalism might say, does not discern the uniqueness of his nation's tradition. A believer in the true faith will similarly object that the outsider insults the faith by turning sacred truth into secular information. The oppressed will ask how the outsider, never oppressed himself, can possibly ever share or even imagine the rage and pain his group feels.

It may well be that the common denominator that accounts for much of the insiders' resentment and suspicion of those outside is the personal and collective pain they feel. It is the pain of peoples who are the victims of modern history, its violence, imperialism, racism, brutality, and destructive greed. They cannot imagine that members of the privileged, dominant, successful classes, ethnicities, or nations could possibly share or understand that pain. It is certainly a major limitation of human perceptions that human beings literally cannot feel each other's pain. But all human beings experience pain. No journey through human existence can possibly be so smooth and easy as to be painless. We all know the pain of loss, disappointment, psychic or physical injury. Such pain is universal and unavoidable. Outsiders, who may well not share the group pain of historical memory as the insider members of a victimized people will do, can at least try to imagine and sympathize. Such imaginative sympathy may seem inadequate. Outsiders can never fully be insiders—that is not my claim.

The outsider thus needs to beware that he does not claim too much, lest he fall into arrogance and insensitivity. Bloke Modisane eloquently and convincingly draws the line against excessive outsider claims to know:

> . . .oppression, poverty and personal humiliation cannot be wholly experienced vicariously, or something one can be intellectual about; one can perhaps only sympathise, nothing more. There are very few things which can be as irritating as the smug understanding of those jokers who profess to know what it would be like to be black in South Africa; it is an arrogant understatement to presume, in the drawing-rooms of their public library homes, to understand the suffocating life in one room. I submit, respectfully, that it is beyond academic comprehension. (*Blame Me On History*. 86–87)

It is a salutary warning. It follows from this, however, that Bloke Modisane himself cannot convey the experience fully. Reading about experience is never the same as the experience itself. But he did write the book, and I believe his effort accomplished something, even for readers who are outsiders. Reading such an account as this, or the powerful, moving poetry of Henry Dumas, or, say, Primo Levi's Auschwitz memoirs, can build some kind of imaginative bridge toward understanding, and that is accomplishing a great deal. The reader, after all, does not want to go through such experiences if it can be helped. But such suffering is all too common in human history, and to expose students to this kind of horrible reality, as vividly as possible, may be some help, however small, at avoiding its recurrence.

Primo Levi wrote for everyone, not just Jews; Bloke Modisane's audience is universal as well, though his book was banned in South Africa for more than twenty years. What outsiders can learn from such accounts is, put simply, enough: enough to discuss, to teach, to compare, to recognize and judge what is good and what is evil. But the claim of *enough* has limits: Primo Levi's suicide, Henry Dumas' death by police bullets (in a case of mistaken identity), or Bloke Modisane's death in lonely exile in West Germany, can all remind us that there are regions of experience that no outsider's grasp toward understanding can ever fully reach.

Such limits, however, do not mean that the outsider should give up or feel put down too easily.

The insider, he says, exaggerates the uniqueness of each group and too readily forgets how much is shared in common humanity. He insists, too, that the secular study of religious phenomena is not an attack on the truth of any faith. Even people's feelings are of limited variety, however much they are experienced within particular group histories. The same range of emotions is available to all human beings however much individual experience may vary.

Besides, if particular insider experiences are so secret, esoteric, and unique that no one else can ever understand, then they are lost to knowledge and become irrelevant to the common experience of humanity. The outsider, however much he may miss of particular group experience, feels able to account for a good deal as a set of variations on the themes within common human experience.

One notes, too, in the history of sociology, how often the marginal person, standing a little outside a society, is able to produce special insights about it. In his study, *The Mind of the Traveler*, Eric J. Leed shows how travelers, quintessential outsiders, have been crucial in providing a basis for human self-awareness. He quotes Georg Simmel on the special powers of the stranger:

> 'he is freer, practically and theoretically; he surveys conditions with less prejudice; his criteria for them are more general and more objective ideals; he is not tied down in his actions by habit, piety, and precedent.' (quoted on p. 63)

These views are, of course, in direct opposition to insider claims. Starting from these premises, the outsider might even claim that, in some ways, it is the insider who does not understand, if he knows only one reality, that of his own group. The outsider has contemplated many groups and societies, albeit from the outside. Without denying the uniqueness of particular experiences in detail, he is in a good position to see what various human groups hold in common and how the unique experiences fall into patterns. In describing a single group experience, he has a good vantage point for explaining and classifying it even if he cannot *feel* the same about it as an insider.

Each insider is a communicant in the one inside group; all other insiders are outsiders to him. That is why the professional outsider's role is a vital one if human beings are ever to understand each other better or to get along better.

If we suppose that a student wants to receive an explanation of the realities of a nation, a religion, or other group, to whom should he turn—to an outsider or an insider? The insider, for all of his conviction of uniqueness or of the truth of his faith, may not be able to communicate these to the student. The outsider, on the other hand, can at least describe the subject in terms the student can understand. He teaches and uses a particular language—the categories that are the universal stock in trade of outsiders for understanding others. The insider, if he is to succeed in communicating his reality to others, must, in fact, master and utilize this language, even as he insists on the special status of his own group.

Thus, the insider needs the outsider's standpoint in order to define himself—as much as the outsider needs the insider to give him the evidence he wishes to interpret.

Above all, the outsider is an educator. In our society, the audience for this education is plural, containing communicants of many different inside realities. The pretensions of no one of them can prevail in the larger mixed group. At times, even, the sacred truth of one may symbolize the oppression of another. One solution is for all to withdraw to their own area and ethnic studies courses and contemplate themselves. But that is unsatisfactory. If our quest for a viable pluralist society is to succeed, such course programs are needed for the general audience. And given that general, plural, diverse audience, the outsider's approach is essential to reveal and build on common experience. The outsider's analysis, precisely because it does reduce unique particularities to general comparative categories, represents the best chance for intergroup communication. If the mixed and pluralist audience does not strive for this kind of common understanding, if each particularity falls back into its own celebration, worship, or affect, then individual groups can only withdraw from the general audience. This implies not only the breakdown of general educational audiences, but the splintering of society itself.

A set of major objections still confronts me. Is my status as a professional outsider really derived from my own ethnic or class background, so that I am advocating the imposition of my insider perspective on others? In this view, the outsider language of analytical categories becomes Eurocentrism, Orientalism, intellectual imperialism, or a particular class perspective. This is the accusation that my assumption of an outsider posture is not a transcending of my particular identity but an expression of it. I am still suspected of being a cultural imperialist.

Various critics have presented such accusations in a persuasive fashion. But their critiques perforce must use the language they are criticizing; the woodsman who cuts down the orientalist tree may himself be sitting in it. Albert Memmi, in order to show the impassable gulf fixed between colonizer and colonized, had to create a privileged position for himself as colonizer-colonized, a unique figure who could understand both sides even as the two sides were locked apart. Jomo Kenyatta's *Facing Mount Kenya*, a famous statement of insider identity, is written in the language of functionalist anthropology.

But it would not do to dismiss these criticisms, for they are a vital part of the process. Outsider views are indeed inadequate, imperfect, and flawed, but they are necessary anyway. They need relentless criticism in order to be effective. The criticisms of orientalism or Eurocentrism are not attacks by aggrieved insiders but rather calls for a more neutral, more universal outside perspective. That is valuable. Insiders, too, rather than ignoring or dismissing outsider accounts of their affairs, ought to give them intense and ceaselesss scrutiny, criticizing them at every point, so that the continuous interplay of insider and outsider views may eventually, however slightly, spread some understanding where ignorance and bigotry now dwell.

The outsider location I have defined may not work for everyone. Teaching is an individual matter, and more than cultural and ethnic background shapes the teacher's capacity. There is also personality and temperament. It is even more difficult to generalize about this and to show how the personal and idiosyncratic can be placed in general terms. All I can do here is describe my own self-assessment and how it influences my classroom demeanor.

To make this examination, to identify personal advantages and disadvantages, special powers of insight or blind spots we may bring to the classroom is, I am arguing, a task for any teacher. To become aware of one's powers or personal limitations is to have a better chance to draw on or overcome them, whether they stem from cultural background or idiosyncrasies of temperament.

I realize, for example, that I chose for my field of study some of the worst areas of intolerance, hatred, conflict, and injustice in the modern world. Yet, in fact, my temperamental preference is for harmony, tolerance, and balance. My interests and my taste are in conflict, and I am aware from this of certain tensions in my teaching and writing. I am conscious of the temptation to clean things up, to portray situations as actually or potentially more harmonious than they really are, or, in a discussion, to show areas of agreement between hotly contested positions. I would count it a success if I made students more willing and more skilled in looking at all sides, more able to discuss even contentious issues within the tolerant and patient rules of academic discussion.

I sometimes wonder whether I go too far in seeking tolerance, patience, balance. Does this tendency really tend to blunt intolerance for things one ought to feel intolerant about? The role of cool-headed observer is a great luxury in a world in which everyone is a participant whether he or she wills it or not, a world in which the classroom is patently not removed and isolated. Does my preference for tolerance leave my students less able to cope with a nasty world?

Does my unwillingness to abandon a liberal-rational outlook leave me less able to understand the societies of conflict I have chosen to study?

For better or worse, these aspects of my temperament do influence how I teach. Again, I try to turn them into advantages, in teaching fields in which controversy rages and any class might contain sharp differences of opinion.

In these circumstances, I still have the position of outsider, and I also need to lead the discussion. Neither role commits me to being neutral. I believe, rather, that my conclusions about an issue should be informed and well-supported but still tentative. I will make the best case I can for a particular viewpoint; but it must be clear that I will also listen to other viewpoints because I am tentative. There should be a tacit agreement between me and other participants that I might learn from them or they from me. The civil atmosphere is important not only to keep feelings from being bruised but, if you will, to allow ideas to be bruised. The tacit agreement allows the discussion to proceed. Breaking the rules should be self-discrediting and tantamount to losing the argument. If my antagonists lose their tempers or attack me personally, I have an advantage in the discussion. If they are unwilling to learn from me, I have an advantage, because I can only improve my case through listening to the contrary case. If I alone consider evidence contrary to my argument, I am the more likely to make the better case. If only my opponents speak in clear language, while I obfuscate, then they are likely to make the better case. If both of us observe the implied agreement to present fairly and to learn if possible, the spirit of mutual inquiry is likely to prosper.

Neither of us need agree to suffer fools gladly. All arguments are not equally to be taken seriously. I am not arguing for relativism; I have discussed my objections to it in chapter 3. The doctrine is sometimes invoked when students express their 'authentic feelings', claiming that these statements of attitude are valid even when not founded on any knowledge at all. Yet neither is it my goal to bring students to agree with my point of view but rather to help them make the best case for their own beliefs, even if they disagree with mine.

I know that in my class students will not receive neatly packaged knowledge or firm and final conclusions. I hope they will get something more exciting. If students have difficulty in accepting the lack of certainty I leave them with, I tell them it is the quest and not the arrival that matters. They have something to look forward to, and perhaps they will keep on thinking.

The reader will have recognized the pedagogy here described. Teacher and students are engaged in a quest for Gandhian truth. In chapter 3 I described this approach as an alternative to relativism and as a means of communicating past the distorting barrier of student preconceptions. Here, Gandhian truth provides a way for the teacher as outsider to pursue an effective discussion, even when a class contains students who claim one or another type of insider knowledge and status.

This kind of classroom is nothing like that of Walter Agard, though it may owe something to his humane and civil spirit. It owes still more to the inquiring, probing, open-ended style of Brentano, and Curtin's commitment to wide-ranging historical inquiry. And, beyond that, it is my response to the ongoing changes in students and the campus environment.

NOTE

1. From the book, *Knees of a Natural Man* by Henry Dumas. Copyright ©1989 by Loretta Dumas and Eugene B. Redmond. Used by permission of the publisher, Thunder's Mouth Press.

5

The Colonizer and the Colonized

> things happen,
> and simply to record them
> is often to deceive,
> is even sometimes to mimic fog,
> the way it's perfectly
> yet inadequately clear about itself.

Stephen Dunn, "Not the Occult," *Landscape at the End of the Century.*[1]

Here I will consider different ways of examining colonial societies and interpreting the colonial situation. These approaches pertain to the histories of the territories ruled by European colonial powers in the nineteenth and twentieth centuries—British India, Dutch Indonesia, French Indochina, or the tropical African colonies of France, Britain, or Belgium.

My intention in this chapter is not to make a contribution to the colonial history of these regions but to examine teaching strategies in the light of the preconceptions of the audience. In any actual class, of course, I would be talking about a historical colonial society and not about an abstract colonial situation peopled by abstract colonizers and colonized. I would not even necessarily present explicit models for conscious application, though this might be done at times. But here I want to make it easier to present the thought processes involved in teaching the subject and keep the essay focused on teaching rather than on the historiography of imperialism and colonial rule —though it is certainly from that historiography that my arguments are drawn. To proceed.

The predominant model by which nearly all students understand the colonial situation is the colonizer-colonized dichotomy. I portray it as follows:

Colonizer
Colonized

This is an extremely simple scheme. The society contains only two elements, the dominant colonizers above the colonized. That is the structure of society. There is no crossing of the line. The main characteristics of the society are discrimination, oppression, and exclusion, and the model brings these elements into sharp focus.

The model suggests that such details as a conflict between imperialists and liberals within colonizer society are not of great importance. All are colonizer supremacists, who should be opposed. The model suggests, too, that whatever divisions exist in colonized society are less significant than the prime cleavage shutting them out of power, resources, and dignity. The programmatic implication here is that if the colonized are not united, they ought to be. The only appropriate line of action for them is implacable opposition to the dominance of the colonizers.

This model is by no means false or useless. It throws a very bright light on certain realities of the colonial situation but this can only be done, as I have stressed earlier, by throwing other relationships into shadow.

There is no subtlety or nuance. The model is static and does not provide for process and change through time. People caught in this situation are only waiting for the final explosion. Yet I believe this model is the most dominant student mindset about colonial rule in Africa and Asia. The pitch of my teaching is set against it throughout. But I have seen more than once, after a full semester of complexity, subtlety, and nuance, all of the final examinations revert back to this simple, primal conflict.

The first point I try to make is about hindsight bias. The colonial situation develops over a number of generations, from contact to annexation by the colonial power, on to the building of colonial institutions, until colonial rule is eventually challenged, and, finally, independence won by the colonized. The consciousness of pancolonized loyalties, I argue, simply did not exist in earlier stages. The local people who may have helped the intruders believed they were only fostering their own group against traditional local enemies. The power and purpose of the colonizer developed only gradually, so that the local people could not possibly foresee what was coming. Therefore, to brand these early collaborators as traitors and turncoats, as the strict colonizer-colonized scheme would have them, seems unjust and unhistorical.

An associated bias of the students is their faith in cultural nationalism. The colonized cause combines, for them, political resistance to the colonizer with unstinted loyalty to colonized culture. Again, I cast confusion and consternation to the believers in this simple scheme. There are two dimensions of interaction between the colonizer and colonized, I argue, a political one and a cultural one: Both develop and change through time. I also argue, here, that the colonizer domination is not totally oppressive, but that a great deal of space exists in which the colonized can make choices.

The inability to imagine that the colonized have a good deal of scope for launching their own initiative and making their own choices is a major feature of the simple colonizer-colonized model. The idea that the colonized have this space is one that students resist with considerable stubbornness, because this notion appears to them to minimize the oppressive nature of colonial rule.

I try to outline these choices in a more complicated typology, which casts light in new areas, even as it might shade some of the areas previously illuminated by the colonizer-colonized model. I present it like this:

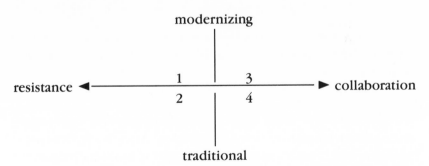

The four quadrants of space represent four possible political-cultural postures for the colonized in response to imperial domination: modernizing resistance, traditional resistance, modernizing collaboration, and traditional collaboration.

As with the colonizer-colonized scheme or any such typology, I need to remind students and myself that the scheme is an ideal type and not reality. But the very discrepancy between the model and reality is what makes it useful. The endless complexity of human behavior in actual social situations can here be sorted, measured, and tested against some fixed categories.

With this caution in mind, I jump in with a broad generalization: In the early stage of colonial society, at the time of conquest and just after, the colonized society tends to be divided between quadrants two and three, between traditional resisters and modernizing collaborators. As time passes and the colonial situation develops we expect a gradual shift away from this pattern until, in mature colonial society, the split between traditional collaborators and modernizing resisters, quadrants one and four, becomes predominant.

Students are uncomfortable with this emphasis on fissures dividing colonized society. Who are the traitors? Are divide and rule tactics being used? Possibly. Or is it simply that all groups within colonized society are gaining whatever advantage they can in a complex situation? In studying actual cases, what we do at this point is to assess the whole complex of circumstances surrounding colonized people as they make choices at a given time. The problem of chronological foreshortening comes up here. Students need to be reminded that the passage of time is just as gradual for historical actors as it is for them. Yet students sometimes think colonized people should already be responding to a reality that was forty years in their future.

In these ways the model helps us to understand collaboration as something besides treachery to the colonized cause, a cause that, in the historical circumstances, did not yet exist.

The model helps students, too, understand that the colonized have cultural choices open to them. The colonizers are powerful and have effective techniques. Collaboration may be a way to gain new techniques and powerful allies; local enemies may for the moment seem more threatening. All of this requires a deliberative examination of the colonial situation as it changes through time.

The original model preferred by the students has been transcended, but it has not been discredited altogether. It could still be useful. Suppose that, as time passes, the colonizer society develops increasingly as a settler regime. Gaining autonomy from metropolitan control, the settlers install an increasingly harsh system of coerced labor, racism, and social exclusion. At this stage, the significance of collaboration changes. The simpler colonizer-colonized dichotomy begins to come into focus, as the result of historical changes. One of the problems of the colonizer-colonized dichotomy was that it was ahistorical and static. Allying it with the dual dichotomies of resistance-collaboration and traditional-modern, we are able to fit it into an analysis of change and development.

The more complicated model thus carries us into a deeper understanding of colonial society. But what are its limitations? We soon find that it becomes strained under the increasing complexity of actual social situations.

My use, here, of the abstractions colonizer and colonized, obscures one important goal of my classes—that is to carry students beyond their view of a colonial society as a kind of moral symbol. By this stage of my argument, I hope that students are developing a sense that the society they are studying is real and not simply an abstraction. If they are gaining a sense of a society in action and process through time, of people with choices, aspirations, hopes, frustrations, people for whom the future is uncertain, people living in history, like ourselves—then these models, whether implicitly or explicitly presented, have taken us some distance. The mindsets of relativism, as noted earlier, and of the colonizer-colonized dichotomy, it seems to me, stand in the way of this ability to perceive another society as a real, human, historical place.

As we continue to look more closely at the society, any African or Asian colony of Europe, the distinctions we have been developing, between traditional and modernizing cultural choices, and between resistance and collaboration, begin to break down. The model carried us beyond the original simple conception, but only so far.

This first becomes obvious when we examine two types of indigenous leaders in the making of cultural choices. The first is the reformer, the second the cultural nationalist. They seem to fit easily enough onto the traditional-modernizing scale. Surely, the reformer is breaking away from his society toward modern options; the students are suspicious of this character. Just as surely, the cultural nationalist is committed to tradition—and allegiance to cultural nationalism is one of the major features of the students' mindset. Both types, however, will prove to be unexpectedly complicated, so much so, that the neat dichotomies we have developed begin to fray out at the edges and then collapse altogether.

Typically, the early reformers were among the first to step out of the traditional society to become familiar with and even comfortable in the culture of the Europeans. Often, their early education had been traditional, but by their teens or even later they received European education. They were therefore at home in both worlds and often acted as cultural brokers between them.

Having grown up precisely in the early stages of colonial rule, they saw the gradually expanding European hold not as an incursion but as a normal situation, which they had to confront and deal with, the context in which they built their careers. Yet even if they did not see the European presence as an aggression to be opposed, that still does not mean they liked it. European presence was perhaps evidence that something was very much wrong with their society, that it could be humiliatingly taken over by outsiders, or very right about European society, that it could take over so easily. In other words, they did not blame the Europeans for the takeover but their own society. This is the social reform premise: "we are ruled by the Europeans," the reformers say, "because we are weak, poor, and divided. To overcome these disadvantages, the society must reform."

My students suspect the reformers of disloyalty to their society, for their failure to oppose the Europeans and their criticisms of their own society. The position of the reformers is indeed a delicate one. They have stepped a little bit outside of the tradition, enabling them to make their critique, but they were brought up in the tradition and still value it.

The choice of all-out westernization is available and some do choose that option, but it is not a general choice. The reformers, instead, choose the strategy of revitalization. What are the things that make the Europeans strong and successful? All over the world, reformers pondered this question, and nearly all came up with a pretty standard list: social and linguistic unity, free deliberative institutions, free thought, science, and a free and educated womanhood. The reason these attributes are not present in their society is that the tradition has decayed! None of the superstitions, inflexibility, tyranny, or other evils which hold society back are really sanctioned by the tradition. The society can progress to the modern world by returning to the purity of their early tradition.

The reformer, as the exponent of this strategy, does not fit very well onto the traditional-modernizing dichotomy. He rather breaks it down. Depending on the precise ingredients of an individual reform program, the revitalization strategy has been defined as spurious, as clandestine westernization, but in other cases it has seemed to be a major remodeling of real traditional life. The reformer is abandoning tradition in the sense of the steady-state, life as it is lived in the society—by returning to tradition! He does not fit on the chart.

My presentation is, if anything, pitched in favor of the reformer, who is a figure that students do not expect to find and distrust instinctively. His existence makes colonial society more complicated. I have to remind students of the slow passage of historical time and of the hindsight bias which makes them blame the social reformers for not sharing the much later consciousness of Frantz Fanon—of not feeling the sharp split between colonizer and colonized because it did not exist in the colony during their lifetime.

The cultural nationalist, usually a later figure in colonial history, breaks down the traditional-modern dichotomy in analogous ways. Like the reformer, he seems to be what he is not. He is proclaiming the tradition, but as a nationalist he is mounting a political movement against European rule. He has reversed the reformer's reasoning. The nationalist premise is: We are weak, poor, and divided because the Europeans rule us. His rhetoric is not in criticism of the tradition but in its glorification. Students are favorably disposed.

Students' commitment to cultural nationalism is hard to account for at first. It is, I believe, an outgrowth of their relativist position, and it is related to their belief in the strict lines drawn between colonizer and colonized. They are cultural nationalists on behalf of the colonized, believing that colonized culture ought to be retained and preserved at all costs. If the colonizers try to spread their culture or induce cultural change, that is simply part of imperialism. If elements of colonized society seek to borrow cultural items or change their culture, that is treachery, collaboration, disloyalty to their cause. The defense of colonized culture is an essential part of the struggle against imperialism.

Such, I have found, is a consistent student bias. Of course, massive evidence against the position makes it untenable, but in teaching the subject and getting students to understand, that evidence is suspect. The teacher is not an insider and therefore suspect also. It takes a more complicated process of argument, not simply a weight of information, to get students to reconsider their position. As many final examination essays have reminded me, it is quite possible for most members of a class to absorb the information without abandoning the untenable position.

How, then, would I pitch my teaching against cultural nationalism? I might accuse students of taking it upon themselves to decide for the colonized what their cultural choices should be. Are not these colonial subjects capable of making their own decisions? In this connection, it needs to be brought out how the cultural choices of the colonized are a mirror image of a cultural policy being pursued by the colonial rulers. And, when they look into this, students discover to their surprise that in many cases, most commonly in the high colonial period, the bias of the colonizers was to preserve indigenous culture and seek traditional collaborators.

In post-independence societies, too, students are surprised at how often a strident cultural nationalism is voiced by regimes which are notorious for neo-colonial subservience and collaboration. Cultural nationalism is beginning to look more dubious and more complicated.

The cultural nationalist position, I can then start to argue, is based on two commonly held conceptual errors. One is the reification of culture. The position depends on the idea that a culture is a fixed definable entity with a real existence and autonomy, so that change introduced into that culture is somehow unnatural and illegitimate. Of course, the fact that many people think of culture in this way is itself important in shaping their choices. But it will not do for us, as observers, to think in this way. Too much that we want to understand gets filtered out in such a model of culture and cultural politics.

A second misunderstanding stems from a confusion between tradition—the cultural practice of the people, life as it is lived through the years—and a posture of ideological traditionalism. People living in the tradition are not normally worried about cultural nationalism but are busy trying to survive and make ends meet, and they are often quite willing to innovate in order to improve their lot. Cultural nationalism is an ideology featuring a set of symbols drawn from traditional life. It is espoused by people, often, whose education and lifestyle have taken them quite far from the tradition. Cultural nationalism, in some cases, is born away from the colony, overseas, in the metropolis, by people seeking an identity, a badge of political allegiance, a rallying cry, and a basis of connection with those who do still live in the tradition.

In this ideological traditonalism, the extent to which real traditional life is being preserved or even advocated is open to doubt.

Cultural nationalist literature is frequently written in the language of the colonizer. Its message is directed as much at the colonizer as at general colonized society.

Its limitations are best understood, again, in terms of the elements that the victims of colonial rule need to oppose colonial rule. They need a power source and an identity source. The colonizers have the power, and resisters will need to borrow, adopt, and master the education, skill, and techniques which are the source of that power. These efforts may take individuals a good distance out of their traditional cultural life. Yet that culture is their identity source. In a way, the quest for power compromises the quest for identity. But to retain unchanged the original cultural base, its religious and explanatory system, is incompatible with the necessary quest for new techniques. Hence, the identity source also compromises the quest for new sources of power. Cultural nationalism is the attempt of those who have left to reestablish their legitimacy as members of the indigenous society; but it can only be a set of symbols, an ideology, not an entire cultural commitment. The new men are committed to new techniques and cannot return fully to the old ways. They are not traditional. They are neo-traditionalists.

But no neo-traditionalist would ever admit that his ideology is only a set of symbols and not a substantial cultural commitment. Therefore, this analysis can only be made by an outsider.

Like the easy, illuminating distinction between traditional and modernizing choices, the resistance-collaboration contrast also begins to break down under the weight of evidence. We can see this in two areas. One is the option to resist the colonizers' takeover with violence; the other in the choices made after colonizer domination is established.

The students are strangely comfortable with the idea of violence in the colonial relationship. Occasionally, when I fail to come up with a sufficiently precise and challenging essay question, I fall back on a kind of roleplaying device, in which I ask students to imagine themselves giving advice to, say, an African king about what to do about European encroachment. I have stopped doing this: students invariably say, "kill the whites." What does this choice represent? It is part of the colonizer-colonized mindset—colonial society, not yet established at this point to be sure, is always in student thinking totally oppressive, thereby requiring total resistance. The students, living in a post-Fanonian world, see Frantz Fanon's revolutionary violence as the one solution to imperialism.

The problem is that the solution the would-be advisors give to the African king is unhistorical. African peoples were courageous and warlike, to be sure, but they did not indulge in gratuitous slaughter. European travellers, traders, and missionaries were, in normal circumstances, relatively safe, even though isolated amid a vast majority of Africans. Furthermore, war was almost invariably forced on Africans, especially after the early phases of imperial advance. Africans understood the odds, the likely costs, and if they had seen the results of military resistance for neighboring peoples, war was not normally their first choice. And they could not anticipate fully the later colonial situation. Frantz Fanon's consciousness was not available to them.

In the consideration of colonial rule proper, a more detailed consideration of cases begins to break down the resistance-collaboration dichotomy. It becomes impossible to tell the difference in specific cases, as collaborators come to seem like resisters in another guise. In a chapter on Central and East African responses to European conquest, Terence Ranger argued that African resisters and collaborators were doing the same thing. Each response, given the nature of the circumstances as understood by Africans, was an attempt to protect and if possible enhance the power and integrity of a given group. Collaborators were men who saw a chance to gain or hold power by cooperation with the Europeans and thus saw no need to resist; resisters were men to whom the Europeans appeared to pose a greater threat than opportunity.

Ranger's point is valuable for the early period. What about the ongoing situation, when Europeans complete the installation of colonial control? Does the initial insight that resisters and collaborators are doing the same thing hold up? In this new period of developing colonial rule, change is extemely rapid. Migrations, new boundaries, new loyalties, new opportunities, new grievances, all contribute to a transformed situation. Individuals can opt out of existing groups and join new ones. The simple resister-collaborator distinction has become too simple. Africans now seem to have as many as five possible options:

1. resistance
2. collaboration

3. symbolic resistance
4. manipulative collaboration
5. neutral activity (which could be defined as resistance)

Symbolic resistance would be activity tolerated or condoned by the administration as a useful pressure cap or listening post. The resister may know how far he can go without getting into trouble. He is, in a sense, a noisy collaborator, though he always runs the risk that the regime can change the rules and round him up, or associate him with extremists. Or he may believe that he is a genuine resister though taken as harmless by the regime, or, again, may even know that his resistance is only symbolic while his followers believe he means business.

Manipulative collaboration is resistance from those whose official position makes them collaborators, such as indigenous bureaucrats in the colonial government. Corruption, petty thievery, undermining of the regime's policies, or merely speaking out to protect the interests of local groups—these are among the many forms the manipulation could take. The situation for this kind of resistance-within-collaboration is always tenuous and unstable. If the practitioner of this strategy goes too far he will become visible and lose his post; if he does nothing he is not a resister. Or, his manipulations may be only self-serving and corrupt and not resistance at all.

Neutral or even collaborative activities can be defined as resistance by a colonial regime. The best example I can think of comes from the history of separatist churches in Africa. The Aladura churches of British ruled Nigeria and the Kimbanguist churches of the Belgian Congo were broadly similar movements arising about the same time, in the early 1920s. Only the Belgians, not the British, decided the new religious movement was a political menace. They persecuted the movement—consequently it became a political menace. Their action itself was what made their diagnosis correct.

Thus, successive sets of models are set up to see what they reveal, only to be knocked down or transcended, starting with that model most allied with the preconceptions of the audience. Step by step, we proceed to closer and closer examinations of colonial society. The process takes in more and more detailed cases. The reality depicted becomes more complicated. Such a series of partial projections of reality from different angles of vision, seems to give me the best chance of carrying my audience beyond their original preconceptions. If I started out with the detailed map straightaway, the audience would be lost, with only their preconceived, simple colonizer-colonized compass to guide them. The burden of detailed information, exceptions, anomalies, and paradoxes, would seem a trackless wilderness. The material would bounce off, leaving the students with their preconceptions intact.

Yet it is not my aim to bring students all to the same conclusions. Rather I want at least to prevent my statements from floating loose with no reference points to predict their impact. Now, I hope my statements are pointed in a particular direction in relation to the audience, lest they have little impact on student thinking.

I hope, too, that by this time I have made everything more complicated. Students' initial belief in the colonizer-colonized world as a fixed reality is, I think, too limiting and too great a handicap to understanding the world. Perhaps I have gotten a few to think in more nuanced ways. Have the students likewise dropped their commitment to cultural nationalism? I do not know. Perhaps they are only a little more confused, but that may well be intellectual progress. I always tell students that if they are too certain of something and it seems fully clear, their position is surely wrong. If they are confused, they may at least be on the right track.

There is no closure in this kind of teaching. My understanding of colonial society is from the outside and it is always, ever incomplete. I hope that the students will not simply adopt my way of looking at things, because I want to keep discussing and arguing with them.

Students are sometimes frustrated. They expect, often, objective, factual accounts. They receive instead elaborate yet partial interpretations. It is difficult to convince them that 'the whole story' is something they will never get, and any account claiming to be complete is illusory.

NOTE

1. Reprinted from the poem "Not the Occult" in *Landscape at the End of the Century* by Stephen Dunn, with the permission of W.W. Norton & Company, Inc. Copyright ©1991 by Stephen Dunn.

6

The Uses of Comparative History

As long as you
know you don't know,
not knowing's not
what hurts,

it's what
you don't know you
don't know that
finally gets
to you, right
in the old
solar plexus.

Philip Booth, "Ganglia," *Relations: New and Selected Poems.*[1]

The theme of comparison runs throughout these essays. What follows is not a systematic survey of comparative history, nor is it a discussion of comparative methods. Such projects would overwhelm this book. Here I only attempt to discuss a few additional ways I have found comparison useful in the classroom.

The subjects I teach lend themselves to it, and the habit of using comparison goes back to my graduate school training. Since those days, comparison has become very much more widespread and accepted, but there are difficulties even now. For undergraduate teaching, a good deal of very fine comparative writing is neglected because it does not fit the subject areas of our courses. Fully developed and extended comparisons seem to burden students with responsibility for two or more bodies of information, and, fact-oriented as they are, they resist and fear this.

Another difficulty is that students have a fixed idea of what comparison consists of and it is difficult to get past this barrier. Generations of American educators have taught junior high students to 'compare and contrast.' Comparison takes care of similarities; contrast deals with dissimilarities. This tradition is a formidable obstacle to students understanding what I am doing when I undertake a comparison. For my purposes, comparison encompasses both similarities and differences, and I believe that is the general practice of comparative history. In considering scores of works of academic comparative history, I have found not a single case in which comparison is limited to the similarities. All consider differences as well as similarities between the cases being compared, as part of the process of comparison. The differences between two cases are, if anything, crucial to the point and value of such comparisons.

We compare, then, not because the two cases are similar but because we want to know how similar or different they are. Comparison is a method of inquiry. To accomplish the inquiry, it would not do simply to recount parallel information about the two cases or compile a list of similarities. What we should do, rather, is systematically to ask the same questions of the two cases. The answers may reveal that the two cases are quite different; to show sharp contrast, one might say, is one possible result of the comparison.

The point that comparison encompasses similarities and differences is persistently difficult for the audience to keep in mind, and the confusion is the source of some of the negative reaction that some comparisons can arouse. A colleague discovered this when he had a class consider a number of cases under the heading, 'Abuse of Power.' "Are you saying that Watergate is like Nazi Germany?" the students asked. The assumption that merely to compare is to assert similarities is one reason that comparisons often cause offense so that the very process of discussion is stopped cold.

Why do I need to make comparisons in a class I am teaching on any given subject, say African or South African history? Isn't the single subject enough of a burden for students to learn? But comparison need not be pretentious or elaborate. It would be rare in class to attempt full length comparisons, in which two entire subjects are set side by side for the full length of a book or a course. Rather, I want to discuss the brief, smaller scale comparative 'asides' that can come up several times in a class—can come up, indeed, frequently enough that they become a major feature of the pedagogy.

This kind of attempt can take several forms. It is, most importantly, a means of taking students from familiar to unfamiliar material. It is also the best way to interpret statements of degree—quantity, intensity, scale, etc. Finally, it serves to take students beyond the particularity of factual information to a discussion of the concepts and categories by which historical information is organized. I will discuss each of these types of comparison below.

Even a brief comparison, to be effective, must be carefully thought through. There are several necessary procedural steps. I must first establish the common categories which are the basis of comparison and work out typologies as a means of organizing data from a set of comparative cases. I must remain aware of the differences between connected cases (in which historical actors might themselves have made the comparison) and unconnected ones (which might be remote from each other in time or place).

My claims for comparison are relatively modest. Comparison is more a means of gaining insight by playing with the material in different ways, rather than a rigorous set of procedures designed to 'establish' social theory. Here is no grand theoretical project, and I would say not 'rigor', but common sense, is what I am aiming at, with the goal of understanding some historical material a little better.

Among the problems and difficulties of comparison the most important is the 'invidious' comparison that might offend someone. Another set of problems stems from claiming too much for comparison. The extent of the claims has to be defined and limited carefully. Yet I will also argue that, in the classroom setting, a comparison can be useful even when it fails to explain anything.

In lieu of examples from the classroom, I will place here a series of brief quotations from historical writing, so that my discussion of the uses, methods, and problems can be attached to some concrete examples:

A. To make my comparisons manageable and meaningful, I have not only shifted topics and angles of vision but even units of analysis. Depending on the time period and the problem at hand, my geographical reference points are the southern United States, the United States as a whole, the Cape Colony or Province of South Africa, or modern

South Africa in its entirety. Similarly, the specific nonwhite groups that are the main object of white supremacist concern and activity vary from chapter to chapter. Attitudes toward Amerindians, Khoikhoi (or 'Hottentots'), Afro-Americans, Bantu-speaking Africans, and Cape Coloreds are each treated within the specific contexts that have given them meaning. The advantage of this topical and segmental approach is that it does some justice to the enormous complexity of race relations in both societies. (Fredrickson, *White Supremacy,* pp. xix–xx)

B. By the time diamonds were picked up and the first gold was discovered, black and white were far on the way to a new society in which both elements were joined indissolubly to one another in the closest of economic relationships. Here finally may be seen the explanation of the failure of South Africa to attract as many immigrants as Canada or Australia. The truth is that she did receive a very considerable immigration. It was an immigration from within. Her immigrants were black. (C.W. de Kiewiet, *A History of South Africa*, 87)

C. The Australians cried 'White Australia,' and the South Africans cried 'White South Africa.' There was no difference between the impulses which expressed themselves in these cries. The difference was between the situation of the South Africans and the Australians. The Australians wished to protect their customary economic and social standards. So did the white South Africans. The Australians believed that the danger to these standards came principally from peoples of a difference race and colour. So did the white South Africans. But the danger which the Australians feared was an external one. Their defence against it took the form of protective tariffs and immigration restriction laws. The danger which the South Africans feared was an internal one. The races which they feared outnumbered them, four to one, within their own boundaries. They tried to protect themselves by the erection of internal barriers, both political and economic. (Hancock, *Survey of British Commonwealth Affairs*, II, Part 2, pp. 63–4)

D. Even so, and terrible as it was, if the slave trade is to be interpreted accurately, it has to be seen in the light of other human disasters. Warfare on other continents was also terrible. So was politically motivated destruction like the Nazi holocaust of the 1940s or the Stalinist destruction of the Soviet peasantry in the course of collectivization in the 1920s and 1930s. Climatic disasters like the most serious sahelian droughts probably killed an even higher proportion of the population over a considerable area, and they still take an enormous toll. So did the epidemiological disasters wrought by European diseases in the Americas in the sixteenth century and the Pacific islands in the nineteenth. The value in making these comparisons is not to apologize for the slave trade, but to help explain how West African societies managed to advance in so many areas of life during the era of the slave trade—and in spite of it. (Philip D. Curtin, *The Rise and Fall of the Plantation Complex* 128)

Fredrickson, writing a general historical comparison of United States and South African history under the general common category of 'white supremacy' is struggling with the problem of units of comparison. His book seems to be one grand comparison, but if he is not simply to list the similarities, the book must be constructed as many smaller units of comparison, each with a point in advancing the argument. Which units are appropriate depends on the immediate data he is treating. For Fredrickson, no single 'correct' comparison exists for any given element in South African society or history.

My experience in classes confirms this. There is, in other words, no single set of correct comparisons to make and no single correct category into which a given historical datum must invariably be placed. What is comparable depends on the purpose of the comparison. In teaching South African history, I find that comparisons with United States history are useful, as a way of moving from familiar to unfamiliar material. Again, I need to stress that differences are as important as similarities.

What comparisons might I attempt to help students understand the history of Africans in South Africa? First, consider the comparison between Africans and Native Americans as two indigenous peoples facing the expansion of European settlers. The experience of European intrusion they share is the common category. Within this common experience, of course, the differences between the two histories are enormous: demographic relationships, disease environments, trade and missionary contacts, and other elements, all revealing sharp contrasts. These contrasts, considered comparatively, provide the class with greatly sharpened explanatory insights. The exercise takes the students from familiar to unfamiliar material and highlights the elements which make two episodes of European intrusion turn out so differently for the victims.

For another segment, I would move to another comparison entirely, one that occurs to most students first. Black South Africans can be compared to African Americans. Both, again, are the victims of racism in white supremacist societies. Both launch movements in protest against their subjugation. Interestingly, in mounting these liberation efforts, they contact and inspire each other's efforts. By the same token, American and South African white supremacists are aware of each other's problems and policies. In a complex double and bilateral interchange, the comparison becomes part of the history itself.

Both comparisons—that with Native American and that with African Americans—illuminate some aspects of black South African experience. And, I should of course add, American history can well be illuminated as well, if such is the purpose of the exercise. But as here I am assuming that my student audience is more familiar with the American case, I concentrate on illuminating the African side as I make these presentations. If the two comparisons are useful to bring about greater understanding, then they are valid—one is not more correct than the other.

Nor do these comparisons exhaust the possibilities. I turn to two much older books, half a century old, for more examples— C.W. de Kiewiet's *History of South Africa: Social and Economic*, and W. K. Hancock's *Survey of British Commonwealth Affairs*.

C. W. de Kiewiet starts with the notable lack of immigrants to South Africa compared to the other lands receiving immigrants at this time, especially the United States, Canada, and Australia. He is taking the reader from these familiar cases to unfamiliar South Africa. And his argument takes an unexpected turn. South Africa did have an immigration, but it was internal. South African blacks are here compared to the immigrants that came from overseas to the other, larger settlements, and this points out something about why South Africa is exceptional in its nineteenth-century development. And black South Africa's absorption into the capitalist economy as a subjugated proletariat is brought into sharp and original focus.

Again, Hancock's comparison is jarring and unexpected. Moving from familiar Australia to explain unfamiliar South Africa (as I believe would be true for most of his readers at the time), he stresses not the racism of 'White Australia' but the protectionism of 'White South Africa.' He pulls the material out of the expected category into an unexpected one. Comparison can be jarring, forcing students to think of the material in new ways.

All of these comparisons, in different ways, get students beyond the facts they are often so interested in, to considering the nature of given historical episodes. There is more than one way of looking at something, and the comparison provides new angles of vision, by placing historical material in new interpretive contexts. Fixed and confidently held mental categories can in this way be given a sharp jolt. Even without any rigorous sociological purpose, my claim is that students' understanding will be enriched.

Philip Curtin's comparative aside puts the slave trade from West Africa into the context of several other well known human catastrophes. The comparison is not carried through and developed. What is its purpose? Here, I believe, is a case of using comparison to measure degree, intensity, and scale. The slave trade was horrible, and students are inclined to assume that the horror was unlimited and total and that to assume less is to trivialize this human tragedy. If this is indeed the audience's assumption, then some comparative perspective is badly needed to provide a context for realistic judgment, but *not* to belittle the slave trade.

When a lecturer or an author makes a statement of quantity or intensity—what I call a statement of degree—the impression the audience will receive is radically variable. Almost more than any other kinds of statements, these float loose, and their impact depends very largely on the expectations of the audience. In the case of the slave trade, Philip Curtin seems to believe, the expectation of readers might be to exaggerate the damage of the slave trade, exaggerate it in fact so greatly that other aspects of African history become inexplicable. In this or any statement of degree, no matter how precisely a quantitative historian may have fixed the statistical accuracy of any number, when all is said and done, the meaning of that number, how it is interpreted, is a matter of the impression it makes. Human beings do not understand the meanings of very large numbers. That is why quantitative statements "float loose".

We may know exactly how many people were killed in a famine or epidemic or military campaign. We may have a good idea of the size of a premodern city or the monetary wealth of a ruling class. But the meanings of the numbers, however accurately determined, are *governed by our expectations*. How much is a lot? The language is impoverished and gives us no help. Very. Very, very. How much is that?

Statements of intensity present similar problems. By these I mean measures of such things as the oppressiveness of a regime, the power of an army, the pitch of loyalty to a certain cause, or many others. Again, when we make such statements, their significance floats loose and is governed by the expectations of the audience. How can we fix and control the impact these statements will have for the audience?

Comparison is the tool that is the most help in this difficulty. It is not a wholly effective tool; it does not pin down statements of degree fully. All Philip Curtin has been able to do in the above comparison is to provide some suggestions for a broader context in which to judge. That is simply the best we can do, for it at least enables us to judge the impact of statements from a second or third point of view. Moving, again, from the familiar back out to the unfamiliar, this kind of comparison may enable us to relate our statement to an area of reality in which students have a better idea of scale and degree.

Still another purpose of classroom comparison, for me, is to pitch my teaching against the positivist bias of many students, discussed in chapter 3. In my classes, students persistently give primacy to facts. To gain data, information, seems to them the key to gaining an education. Furthermore, they believe that words are—or should be—quite rigorous designators for the objects in the world. This is, at least, my hypothesis to explain part of the pattern of misunderstanding I encounter in my classes. And I can think of many reasons in the society and in the American educational experience why it would be true. It makes sense to me. I act on it, then, by pitching my teaching against positivism. Comparison, again, is a useful tool here.

One conspicuous aspect of the positivist bias of students is the belief that the common historical concepts, such as nationalism, imperialism, racism, colonialism, are or represent objective and fixed realities. To them, they are words with 'correct' definitions. Our senses, it seems to them, perceive these things; that is how we know about them. One kind of comparative exercise is useful here: to work out a set of case studies under one of these headings, cases of imperialism, or race relations situations, or colonial situations.

When we assemble the various cases under the heading of, say, imperialism, some interesting things begin to happen. No two cases are alike, and we can now try to divide the cases into types. We may have some cases that are too different or too anomalous—perhaps these cases are something else, not imperialism. To decide this, we have to establish some outside boundaries for the term *imperialism* and to move some of the cases outside the boundaries. This requires establishing imperialism as one type of some larger category, say *domination* or *aggression*. But our greatest discovery is that we never agree on a final definition of the term. What we may be able to agree on is that some definitions are more useful than others, as we play back and forth from the specific cases to the general category, from inductive to deductive reasoning.

This kind of comparative exercise in a class tends to elicit a lot of student participation. That itself can be valuable, because it delays closure. I have spoken of the way my statements can float loose, to be pushed in many different directions. One of the most common things that happens is that students take a contingent statement to be a final one, to be written down, colored yellow, and memorized. My pitch is to bring them up short if I can.

As positivists, they believe that their understanding of things is rational, objective, and correct. They do not consider other ways of thinking, for other ways of thinking are incorrect and not worth considering. (This may seem to contradict their belief in relativism. But relativism, as I have argued in an earlier chapter, serves as a way of dismissing other ways of thinking and *not* considering them.)

The placing of units of reality into unexpected comparative categories provides a way of making the students think about thinking rather than simply about the information. There are many ways of thinking about any given historical episode or situation, I am suggesting in these comparative forays. In different contexts the same body of information takes on sharply altered significance.

Thus, the series of comparisons of South African blacks with Native Americans, African Americans, European immigrants, and the Asian would-be immigrants excluded from Australia.

Another set of historical cases I have enjoyed using as a teacher (even as I discover new angles for myself) involves the careers of nineteenth-century British colonial governors. They were peripatetic, in the course of their careers holding office in as many as six or seven colonies. Men such as Sir Arthur Gordon, Sir George Grey, Sir John Pope Hennessy, Sir William Jervois carried their accumulated experience as baggage from post to post. They were living experiments in comparative studies, as they applied their experience of one colony to solve the problems of another. Their mistakes and successes provide the best examples I have found of what I would term the *comparison of connected cases*. They fit nicely into the subject matter of a single course.

More difficult to fit into a historical class are the comparisons in which the units are widely separated in time or space—Moses I. Finley's analysis of ancient and modern slavery, or Leo Spitzer's *Lives in Between*, which analyzes marginality and assimilation in specific families in Austria, Brazil, and Sierra Leone in the nineteenth century. Spitzer's sophistication in setting up and justifying his project is worth noting:

> By the mid-nineteenth century, individuals in all these families had become engaged in the process of assimilation: they were traveling on a road opened up and, in part, cleared for them by the beginnings of commercial and industrial modernization, and by the legal, social, and economic changes associated with the emancipation of slaves, minorities, and various other subordinated groups. As such, these individuals were personally involved in a process of social change taking place on several scales at once, from the family to the global political economy. For them, as for so many others, this process seemed to offer the possibility of mobility into, and identification with, a class-based social order. The cultural values and standards of this order were in large part defined and set by the most energetic and economically powerful group in the industrializing world: the bourgeoisie. (Leo Spitzer, *Lives in Between*, 6)

Spitzer here juxtaposes three widely separated cases and takes them out of the usual 'national' or 'regional' boxes and reminds us that the forces and processes shaping these lives are worldwide. Without moving all the way into a theory-bound historical sociology, he transcends the usual concern for the unique body of historical facts of a single society. Here, comparison moves not from the familiar to the unfamiliar but from parochial to global contexts and explanations.

Spitzer's work goes against a traditional view that historical knowledge advances by detailed archival work on small, 'feasible' topics, basing his work instead on the ideal of *span*. Some would question whether such a vast area can be mastered by one scholar. But what if the small local archive does not contain answers to the questions the historian wants answered but offers evidence only for a pseudo-local explanation? Deeper knowledge of, say, the Brazilian archives would not help Spitzer, when the forces shaping the lives of his subject family are coming from elsewhere. The explanatory power of span is, then, a further benefit of the comparative approach.

Beyond the information involved in any of these comparisons, it is the activity itself, no matter what units are being considered, that can open up new intellectual vistas. I try to tell students that their way of thinking is contingent, that they have a certain mental framework. They are not perceiving objective reality but interpret received data in terms of this framework or 'mazeway'. They are comfortable and learn most readily when they are receiving data that fits nicely into their mazeway and confirms it. New categories and juxtapositions call their framework into question. That can hurt. That can be annoying, and it may be one reason, occasionally, why comparisons cause offense. The positive and objective qualities that students give to their mental categories and concepts are challenged, with the goal not of destroying them but of making them more flexible and useful.

Despite all of these uses, some comparative gambits may offend someone and be an actual obstacle to understanding. The invidious, political comparison is, indeed, a standard way of insulting opponents in international politics. It is usually clear that this is the purpose of the comparison, but many people tar all comparisons with this same brush. The invidious comparison usually takes the form of an assertion of similarities, there being no real interest in an analytical assessment of differences and context. The most common form of the abusive political comparison is to compare something or someone with Hitler, the Nazis, or the Holocaust. These cases almost cannot be used at all in analytical comparisons without raising hackles.

Frank Chalk and Kurt Jonassohn at the Montreal Institute for Genocide Studies have recently attempted a full-length comparison and have followed comparative procedures broadly similar to the ones I have been describing here. They place their cases under the common general category 'genocide,' and they establish a typology of genocide. They have, in other words, constructed a comparative inquiry and could not have distanced themselves more effectively from the common use of holocaust comparisons as a form of political mudslinging. One can predict, anyway, that critics of Chalk and Jonassohn will say that the Nazi genocide of the Jews is 'not comparable' to anything else—even though such critics must have made a comparison of some sort to come to that conclusion.

Having said that, I will here consider two earlier uses of the Nazi-Holocaust comparison, one of them fairly successful, and neither of them particularly likely to cause offense, though I could be wrong about that.

In Stanley Elkin's book, *Slavery* there is an extended comparison between slavery in the American south and Nazi concentration camps. Whether one agrees with Elkins' conclusions or not, the comparison is done effectively. Noting the reputed harshness of American slavery in an implicit comparison with other slave systems, Elkins then places the slave regime and concentration camps under the common category, 'total institutions,' which he defines at length. He goes on to show the psychological damage revealed in studies of concentration camp victims and suggests that the existence in some slaves of a "sambo" personality may stem from a similar kind of personality damage.

Historians of slavery have moved away from the assumption that slavery was anything close to a 'total institution.' Elkins' comparison, however, still seems to me effective. If we remember that the claims are limited, that his comparison does not prove anything but rather provides a suggestive idea for interpreting one aspect of slavery, showing a pattern that could exist at times—then this comparison, dated as it is, is still valuable, still worth considering.

Consider the following Holocaust comparison:

> The "final solution" to the Communist problem in
> Indonesia was certainly one of the most barbaric acts of
> inhumanity in a century that has seen a great deal of it;
> it surely ranks as a war crime of the same type as those
> the Nazis perpetrated. (Gabriel Kolko, *Confronting the
> Third World*, 181)

Here, the use of the comparison is not to measure a statement
of degree or quantity, although it seems so at first. It is a statement,
rather, of moral indignation, and it equates CIA acts with those of
the perpetrators of the Holocaust. The statement does not, it seems
to me, help to measure the degree of seriousness of the anti-
Communist purges in Indonesia. Admittedly, it is only an aside and
not a developed comparison, but such asides are the most common
forms when we make a comparison with the limited purpose of
fixing our impressionistic statement into a more concrete mold.

The reason, I believe, that Kolko's statement is ineffective is that
holocaust comparisons in general have lost their force and value
as comparisons through overuse in politically charged rhetoric. The
key word in the quotation is *type*. Kolko is asserting that the
Indonesian massacres and the Holocaust fit within a common
category, but only a generalized one of twentieth-century barbaric
inhumanity or of 'war crimes.' The statement is only an assertion
and does not present any comparative analysis.

But if Kolko's comparative aside failed, that is all right. It is
perfectly acceptable to a classroom comparison, too, to fail and break
down. As Josephine Miles wrote, 'What learning allows for is the
making of error/Without fatality.' ("Center," *Collected Poems* 234)[2]

There is still value in the intellectual exercise, and the failure
may provide negative evidence pushing us toward something else
that might work. Even if two cases are remote in time, space, and
culture and seem distinctly unpromising, why not try? A well known
proverb avers that one cannot compare apples and oranges. Why
not? I have seen useful and serious comparisons between Be-bop
and tumbleweed, and between Neo-Hinduism and pizza pie. My
inclination is toward making the attempt at a comparison, even when
the outcome is uncertain.

Having said all this, there is still something more to the educational value of comparison. I am struggling with it and trying to pin it down, this further reason why the habit of making comparisons and, really, thinking comparatively all the time, is an important skill, beyond the development of more or less formal and academic historical interpretations.

In the end, comparing different societies keeps us in mind of common humanity, which the worldwide din of strident political propaganda tends to make us forget. At the broadest level, humanity is the common category, against which we can test the cultural and temporal specifics of each society that provide the raw material for most historical explanations.

We do not know everything about human affairs; the best informed of us are deeply ignorant, yet we, perforce, must think and act anyway, pretending that our incomplete information is complete enough to provide a basis for these activities. But our ignorance in fact leaves us vulnerable to the dehumanizing forces of political debate around the world. The habit of comparison, I speculate, may enable us to protect ourselves.

And to cope with the unpredictable world as events unfold. In a possibly apocryphal anecdote, I am told that Zbigniew Brzezinski brought comparative history to the Carter White House. As the Iranian revolution proceeded and the Shah's regime teetered toward collapse, Brzezinski urged White House staffers to read Crane Brinton's *Anatomy of Revolution* so that they could understand what was happening and anticipate the likely outcome. I hope the story is true, though if Brzezinski hoped to use comparative history as a vehicle for *controlling* events, he was going farther than I am prepared to think is possible.

My claims would be somewhat more modest—that the habit of comparison provides us with a way of imagining an unfamiliar subject and accounting for what we do not know about it. Again, we are moving from the familiar to the unfamiliar. It seems a dangerous procedure, but, remember, we are not presuming similarities. We are setting questions, not listing answers.

Comparison, you might say, enables us to live with our ignorance. When there are gaps in our information, the habit of comparison enables us to leave space for new knowledge to fit in. In terms of the conceptual organization of our thinking, it helps us to remain flexible, prepared to fit data into new categories, and reorganize our knowledge in new forms.

NOTES

1. "Ganglia," from *Relations: New and Selected Poems* by Philip Booth. Copyright ©1986 by Philip Booth. Used by permission of Viking Penguin, a division of Penguin Books USA Inc.

2. Reprinted from the poem "Center," in the book *Collected Poems, 1930–83*, by Josephine Miles. © Josephine Miles 1983. University of Illinois Press. Used by permission of the publisher.

7

Teaching a Racially Sensitive Subject

> He continues quick and dull in his clear images;
> I continue slow and sharp in my broken images.
>
> He in a new confusion of his understanding;
> I in a new understanding of my confusion.
>
> Robert Graves, "In Broken Images", *Collected Poems*.

I approached my teaching of South African history in spring 1984 with some trepidation. I had taught the course numerous times before and would teach it again. But the controversy over the case of Professor Ernest Dube was just then raging on the campus. He had allegedly stated "Zionism is racism," though the actual assertion was made as an essay topic to which students were to respond. Still, people took offense.

That year, we all argued about that case. Whatever its merits, which are not my topic here, I took the matter personally. I recalled the spring before how, in discussing European racism, I described the old view that Africans had preferred Islam because "it was a simple and undemanding religion," therefore suitable for simple people. I believed that I had very thoroughly labeled this view as an illustration of European racism in the imperialist era. But after class, I heard students talking on their way out of the building: "He said that!? We have to do something." I waited for the students to catch up, and straightened the matter out then and there. Once they had gone public to expose the racist professor, the thing would have taken on a life of its own and there could have been no calling it back—as we were finding out that year in Professor Dube's case.

I began to realize that teaching such a controversial subject as South African history might be positively dangerous, and I began to discern a more general problem. When the world's most violent controversies encroach into the academic environment, our traditional style of discussion becomes more and more threatened. Nor is there any retreat away from these controversies. They are important; they are what we should be dealing with in the social science classroom.

One of my reactions to the controversy over academic freedom and responsibility at Stony Brook is ironic. I find that my teaching is at times criticized not for my espousing of a definite political line but for my seeming failure to do so. What follows is my answer to these criticisms.

The study of South African history raises issues of injustice, oppression, and social conflict as deep and compelling as any in the contemporary world. The Apartheid legislation may now be repealed, but these issues are still pressing, in South Africa and elsewhere. To be a student of South African history is to come face to face with one's own values and with the question of one's own commitment to justice in the world. But the answer for each student of the subject will be different and will be made at different times.

There are many students who, from the first day of class, will address the issues of South African history with mature conviction, seeking effective ways to commit themselves to activist roles. They are, and have a right to be, people whose minds are determined on this subject.

Others by contrast enter the course as novices, knowing little or nothing of historical or contemporary South Africa. However hot the topic, they need to master the material before they can consider any activist commitment, if they ever do. In the past, I have had representatives of both these groups, and of intermediate groups, all in one classroom at the same time.

This great variety in the audience has important implications for the effective presentation of the course. The course is at once an introductory survey of a large subject and therefore selective and incomplete. I lack the time, I lack the knowledge, to say everything; as it is, the numbing accumulation of unfamiliar material can be overwhelming.

I do have to leave a good deal out, and I am sometimes questioned about my omissions. South African history is full of the most brutal crimes and inhuman atrocities. Inevitably I omit something that a student regards as particularly telling. I can only answer that I make a full enough selection to make the point. I admit to cleaning up the subject a good deal: I have no wish to make people sick.

I would argue too that it is not any particular selection of facts that will give the course its bite, but rather how the information I use is organized. I try to make the course conceptually advanced, with the burden of studying a variety of historical and sociological viewpoints added to that of becoming acquainted with the actors and events of a particular historical society.

To accomplish all this, the method must be one of inquiry, of a seeking for understandings of the subject, so that no single interpretation is being imposed. What, it is asked instead, are the implications or consequences of various interpretations of the history?

In class, such an approach can cause at least two problems. Those who already have their own understanding may sometimes feel impatient with the academic, uncommitted tone of the course. Too often, it must be said, they want to hear what they already agree with. On the other hand, all students but especially the beginners in the subject, may sometimes mistake statements made as exploratory inquiries to be the concrete, instructor-backed inter-pretations they seek and expect. Too often, in other words, they want to be told what to think. It is my perverse pedagogical preference to frustrate both kinds of expectation.

Both groups are too impatient. The course develops in slow compexity over sixteen weeks, just as South African history develops in slow complexity over four centuries or more.

But one can see good reason for impatience. South Africa under Apartheid has been a caldron of injustice and struggle, and here is a professor analyzing, trying to understand, weighing, qualifying. Academic treatment runs the risk of seeming lifeless and antiseptic; patient analysis can seem euphemistic, condoning, empty of relevance. A patient and balanced presentation in the face of injustice can seem a kind of taking sides, and a detached style can destroy the sense of caring. It is as important to avoid this error as to avoid partisan bias. In fact I do not undertake to be either balanced or objective. I will say all sorts of personally biased things, but I do not expect to impose, or even to offer, a consistent interpretive line. I expect disagreement. In my experience, one of the best ways to make up one's mind is with that quick flash of insight: "Aha! That is exactly what I disagree with."

Bias, yes; but the tone is still to be that of a considered inquiry. The process of study really precludes vituperation, name calling, or a pep rally atmosphere. For those seeking to be active against South African injustice, the class is a time for background preparation and not activism. Less effective places to demonstrate one's commitment may exist than a Stony Brook classroom, but not many. Philip Rieff underlines this point perhaps even more emphatically than I would:

> It is our duty to protect and nurture, in our academies, a few enclaves within which to practice an inhibiting subtlety, to think in something like late Jamesean sentences. If we are not allowed indirections, slowly ordered, if we must serve some program, one side or another, then the academy has no unique service; it is least fit of all institutions to take stands or rationalize them. (*Fellow Teachers*, 52)

By way of compensation, the study of the subject even for the well informed ought to yield a payoff for the potential activist, through a sharper understanding of how the system works, and greater knowledge of the successes and failures of those who have gone before.

All the issues that arise over the tone and style of classroom presentation arise also over the question of assigned reading. Hundreds of books on South Africa are available: academic studies, activist polemics, apologias, fiction, memoirs, travel, and journalism. Only a limited amount can be assigned. My typical assigned reading for the course would include an academic textbook, and fiction or memoirs by Englishmen, Afrikaners, and Africans, to serve as a basis for paper assignments. I am often asked why I do not use some of the many trenchant and informative activist writings, rather than a sterile academic text? All the points made above may here be repeated in this connection. In addition, the limited reading assigned is a kind of invitation. The way to get into the subject is to keep on reading and to eat, sleep, and drink South Africa—to immerse oneself in the subject. The course usually hooks a few students in this way.

The central and sensitive issue of the course is racism. The entire course, I hope, is a condemnation of racism. But within the course admittedly this may be less obvious. It may seem a strange request to ask people to *understand* racism rather than condemn it. This point is this: South African society, going through several transformations, has manifested racism in a great variety of ways. White domination has been maintained by a variety of mechanisms. In studying the evolution of South Africa's racial system, then, there is more to do than condemn. The different structures prevailing at different times might be alike in their injustice, but the other distinctions between them are still worth making. Each system had its own list of beneficiaries and victims, each its own capacity for change or survival. Understanding is a different activity from condemning, more difficult, requiring more patience. One who would condemn effectively had better understand first.

There are, too, compelling rival historical interpretations of the origins and development of the South African racial system. Which of these one accepts has among other things important implications for the activist's choice of appropriate action against the regime. These implications are in a way more interesting than the possibility that one interpretation is correct—about which agreement is unlikely in any case. The historical interpretations, like the sociological models, have to be presented, examined, and assessed. But to present them is not to praise them.

The very language of South African history raises problems of the sensitive presentation of material about race: the language of the regime is the language of racism. The Apartheid system divided the population into racial groups, and to talk about such groups is to acknowledge their existence. If that is necessary, it is also necessary to disclaim acceptance of the government's racial designations as legitimate.

This very argument arose, for example, over the question of the 'colored' people. One point of the Black Consciousness movement of the 1970s was to draw all non-whites into a single anti-Apartheid alliance and to form a positive and unified identity rather than a residual category of the disadvantaged. When I mentioned the 'colored' group, there was objection from the audience that the group did not exist at all except by the force of South African law.

Another aspect of South African terminology that can cause difficulty is the evolving series of names Europeans have given

Africans through the course of South African history—Kaffir, Native, Bantu, Non-White. Aside from the arrogance inherent in this unilateral dubbing, the names have, one by one, through association with injustice and disparagement, become racist in connotation. Fashions also simply change. A usage in the nineteenth century, while racist in itself, might not have had the ugly connotation that the same usage would acquire in the twentieth century. In discussing South African history, such names have sometimes to be used in an analytical or historical context. But the racial disparagement involved in these usages occurred in South African history. In the Stony Brook classroom, such terms are used for documentary purposes—and *not* to repeat the insult.

This is an important point especially when, in studying the racist fabric of South African history, we put racism on display by quoting racist statements or assigning racist readings. These are documents to be analyzed; quotation does not involve approval. Here is a potent source of misunderstanding, as the sight of racism sets off an understandable response. All I can do is to enjoin people to listen carefully and consider the source.

Can the scholar and the activist coexist, in the same person or in the same classroom? I am perhaps simply asking for forebearance on the part of activists, while I make an intellectual game out of the subject, as one student commented.

Admittedly I am teaching something more than South African history. I am actively pushing a line: the values of academic inquiry. These values include, for me, the patient consideration of complex data, the slow movement toward evershifting tentative conclusions for which the evidence is never all in, the continued willingness to learn from a new perspective as a test of one's own angle of vision.

Do such values, I have been asked, not themselves make a strong and effective political commitment to justice impossible? Are they not paralyzing in their wishywashy tolerance? My answer is no. Scholarship or activism has each its own sphere. The academic sifting and winnowing can be a prelude to committed political campaigns. Gandhi believed that the truth he could achieve was ever partial, tentative, and subject to revision; but he was willing to strive for his currently existing vision of truth with unlimited commitment and devotion.

But while it may be possible to bridge the gap between activist and scholarly values, it is certainly not easy. The contrast between the two sets of priorities remains deep. Robert Graves' poem, "In Broken Images," quoted at the beginning of the chapter, describes nicely the contrast I have seen between the scholar and the activist. The activist has firm and decided convictions; the scholar remains tentative and is ever in search of new evidence. The activist understands the subject; the scholar wants to understand. The activist wants the scholar to state his convictions and act on them. The scholar wants the activist to keep her mind receptive to additional evidence. Both, I would say, should take the other's advice seriously.

My own activist project is to defend scholarly values in a dangerous world. That is my first priority. Along with Robert Graves, I find the attempt to understand the world through my broken images more satisfying than the other man's success in finding clear images.

8

On Understanding the South African Freedom Struggle

most cruel, all our land is scarred with terror,
rendered unlovely and unlovable;
sundered are we and all our passionate surrender
but somehow tenderness survives.

Dennis Brutus, *A Simple Lust*.[1]

When Nelson Mandela's daughter Maki was at Stony Brook as a Distinguished Lecturer early in 1991, she leaned to her neighbor at dinner: "Can I ask you something? What is Afrocentrism? People have been asking me about it ever since I got here."

In another incident from about the same time, a mixed South African group toured the United States. They reacted with shock and consternation when the white members of the group were excluded from Minister Farrakhan's temple. "This would never happen in South Africa," they said.

Again, recently, a colleague noted to his class that Namibia was the last African country to receive independence. No dependent territories remained. There was murmuring, and several hands went up. "What about South Africa?" someone asked. "The South African struggle is not for independence," my colleague said. More murmuring. Many students were a little suspicious.

One final anecdote: The psychologist turned musicologist Helen Kivnick visited South Africa in 1984. The fruits of her research were two albums of African singing and a book on African music in South Africa. But on her return to the United States, she was in deep trouble. Many people denounced her for breaking the UN-sponsored cultural boycott, even though the boycott never applied to scholarship of this sort. Such accusations were ignorant and muddled at best. A boycott used to silence the voices that Helen Kivnick enabled us to hear would be an indiscriminate and ineffective instrument indeed.

These anecdotes are evidence of sharp contrasts between American and South African attitudes and circumstances. They suggest that an interpretation of South Africa filtered through American concerns, priorities, and alliances might be seriously distorted.

The comparisons I make between South Africa and the United States must be framed carefully. The parallels between the United States and South Africa are at times so obvious as to be dangerously misleading. Merely listing the obvious similarities will not work. There is a kind of sea change in the values of some words, and the differing historical experiences of the two societies need to be highlighted, not ignored, in making these comparisons.

The model students use in making the comparisons is, again, the colonizer-colonized dichotomy, with a racial focus, the blacks against the whites. Distortions of understanding stem both from false parallels with the United States civil rights struggle and from the notion that South Africa, being in Africa, is a dependent 'colony.' Since this is where students are located, I will start with this model, moving through the gradually more complicated steps I have outlined in a previous chapter.

A close study of the African National Congress, its history and its policies, is the key to persuading students that fine distinctions, subtlety, and nuance, are needed to get past the superficial level to a deeper understanding of South Africa's history.

The ANC waged armed struggle for twenty-nine years and still pursues its goals with militant determination. In the atmosphere of tough negotiations and recurring strikes and boycotts since 1991, South African affairs are hard to decipher. We must not lose sight of what the ANC struggle is about. It is not and never was a black struggle against whites but rather the struggle of an ANC-led alliance against the racist system of white domination.

The ANC has adhered unwaveringly to an inclusive, universalist, color-blind ideal, "that South Africa belongs to all who live in it, black and white," in the words of the 1955 Freedom Charter, still the fundamental statement of ANC goals. This document was drafted by the Congress Alliance, a coalition of groups representing all races, and many of the framers were accused of treason for espousing its ideals. These are the ideals, as he eloquently stated in his 1964 Rivonia Trial Statement, for which Nelson Mandela would devote his life and for which, if need be, he was willing to die.

This ANC posture is in sharp contrast, it seems to me, with a good deal that is going on in the United States, where ethnic nationalism, cultural separatism, and even linguistic varietism are now prominent, even if fairly mild and muted by the standards of other world regions. Why is the ANC stance in South Africa exceptional in this way?

For the answers, we need to consider two periods: the period of the Apartheid regime proper, from 1948 to 1989, but including the segregationist trends that prepared the way for Apartheid, going back to 1913 and even earlier; and the period of missionary acculturation and Cape Liberalism that flourished in extensive parts of South Africa from the 1830s to the 1930s.

The earlier period was the period of conquest, loss of African resources, and eventual proletarianization. But it was also the period when a fairly extensive African elite was trained. In the Cape Colony and Province between 1852 and 1936, Africans could vote on the common roll, subject (until the system was watered down) to the same tests of literacy and property that all voters had to meet. 'Colored' people (the mixed race group) retained this franchise down into the 1950s.

The missionary education was elitist, paternalistic, and assimilationist, with full assimilation to be achieved by the most leisurely gradualism. But, following a strict definition of the term, not racism but cultural arrogance was the basis of this policy. The assumption was that Africans were fit and capable of adopting Christianity and the 'superior' culture and language (English) that went with it. It was from the Africans who had been through this educational system, who enjoyed the limited political rights of the Cape system, and who aspired for their extension, that the ANC leadership emerged.

This, then, was the system that the Afrikaner National Party would attack and eventually destroy, and their motivation was at least partly to check English influence. Their policy of Apartheid was specifically meant to thwart those African aspirations that the liberal system had allowed and fostered. Apartheid was based on a frankly acknowledged racist doctrine in a way that the old missionary liberalism was not. The doctrine held that to assimilate Africans to European culture was to tamper with God's handiwork. In any case, Africans were not capable of becoming Europeans. They made good Africans and should therefore "develop along their own lines." The Afrikaner theorists of Apartheid envisaged African nations parallel to their own and living separately. Separate ethnicity was forced on Africans as part of the oppressive system, as the Apartheid regime attempted to 'unscramble the egg' of African society.

There were two ways for the leaders of the ANC to respond to this. They could accept the premise of separateness and assert a counternationalism, even one that made use of the categories imposed by the regime. They could in this way take up the imposed identity and glorify it. Or, they could retain the old aspirations, insisting on an ideal of common citizenship and common access to a universalist education and competition in a unified arena of opportunities. They chose the latter option and have stuck with it doggedly.

However much the Africans' former English liberal mentors had been arrogant and patronizing themselves, however much they had let the Africans down, the choice was never in much doubt.

In some forms, ethnic particularism was simply too obviously discredited by association with the racist regime, but a more generalized 'Africanism' was still a possibility. There was, in fact, a consistent undercurrent of 'Africanism' from the 1940s. This ideology took the position that South Africa was an African country in which Africans should work out their own future and define a distinctly African identity.

But Anton Lembede, the first exponent of Africanism within Congress, died young, and Nelson Mandela gave up this line of thought early. The Pan Africanist Congress, led by Robert Sobukwe, split off from Congress in 1959 because they feared too much Communist—and white—influence within the Congress Alliance. They called instead for common cause with newly independent African states and mass action within South Africa. But the PAC was badly disrupted in the 1960s, and the Black Consciousness movement led by Steve Biko in the 1970s was based on self help and pride more than separatism. In fact neither the PAC nor Black Consciousness advocated in their early years an all-out black domination, nor did they foment anti-white feelings.

It is true, however, that today's PAC and the Bikoist AZAPO (Azanian People's Organization) have maintained the armed struggle into 1993, with the slogan, "one settler, one bullet." Whether this represents, finally, an all out anti-white campaign, or a temporary tactic in the struggle, is difficult to judge. These organizations are, in any case, small groups, dwarfed by the much more powerful ANC.

These groups could pose a threat to the common society if they succeed in recruiting the youth. The undercurrent of Africanism has persisted and is still present. During the many years the ANC was banned, the idea was taken up by each younger generation. But most people outgrew it as they matured. One reason for this abandonment of Africanist or separatist ideologies, apparently, is the persistence of ANC training, acquired in a very curious way. After the long early prison years in the rock quarry, the conditions of his imprisonment eased enough that Nelson Mandela was able to run a clandestine seminar in political ideology on Robben Island. Generation after generation of detainees were trained by him, and the United Democratic Front of the 1980s, led by a number of graduates of the seminar, held firmly to the ideals of the Freedom Charter. The training of the 'comrades' in Tanzania and the front line states had the same result.

Another factor in shaping the ideological posture of ANC leadership today may be the social results of the "Botha reforms." The Botha years, 1979–1989, are best known for their savage repression and violence. But a lot else was quietly going on. Early on, Botha asked Afrikaner and other businessmen how the regime could survive in the face of international disapproval. They told him they needed educated African workers, prosperous black consumers, African unions to negotiate with, and a whole new African middle class. To a significant extent, not altogether because of government policies, these kinds of changes occurred in this period.

Local municipalities, in the meantime, were quietly dropping many of the annoying practices of petty Apartheid.

But once all of these changes had been allowed, the rest of the system could not be saved, even by unlimited force.

It seems to me a commonsense expectation that the enormous burden of Apartheid and the frenzied violence with which the regime over many years reacted to challenges would leave little basis for a common society. This expectation may still be confirmed: the ANC quest for a common society could yet falter. (As an aside, I must add here that the wrecking of hopes for a common society through a resurgence of white tribalism is at least as likely.)

But the course of events has so far contradicted this 'common sense of the matter,' that having suffered so much, Africans would be almost bound to hate the whites and wreak vengeance on them. Decade after decade, and consistently, by far the most powerful trend of the African freedom movement has been to uphold the doctrine of the Freedom Charter. The aspirations of the first Secretary of Congress, Sol Plaatje, who translated several Shakespeare plays into Setswana, are seemingly being fulfilled.

Still, why is Anglophone education not considered part of a 'cultural imperialism'? I can think of four reasons: (1) it is the path of career opportunity in South Africa; (2) it is this path that the policy of Apartheid most specifically cut off, and it was natural for the struggle against Apartheid to demand its reopening and extension.

(3) In the South African context, furthermore, English is neutral. It is not the nationalist tongue of an exclusivist *volk*. Afrikaans is identified as the language of oppression, and insistence on English has even, at times, served as a means of defiance and protest. English is neutral, and it is imperial, representing not only opportunity and access but universality. It is the basis of the persistently held aspirations for a common society and the linguistic medium of that society.

What about the question of 'African identity'? (4) Most educated Africans are tri-lingual, and African language and culture are available to them. In this sense, the maintenance of an African identity is simply not a problem in South Africa. Africanness is a comfortable ongoing reality and therefore need not be asserted through ideological posturing. I would in fact argue that African traditional values may well be one source of the ANC's inclusionist doctrines and that to make them a basis for separatism would be to betray them.

The ANC is, in short, not struggling for independence from colonial rule in the sense that many American observers think. And Helen Kivnick's work was welcomed and supported by the Africans she visited, who included prominent leaders of the United Democratic Front. They never told her she should go away and boycott them.

These considerations go some way to explain, in addition, why the term *Afrocentricity* simply did not resonate with Maki Mandela, or, for that matter, why the exclusion of white visitors from a Black church was something that "would never happen in South Africa."

NOTE

1. Excerpt from "Somehow We Survive" from "Sirens Knuckles Boots & Other Early Poems" from *A Simple Lust* by Dennis Brutus. Copyright ©1973 by Dennis Brutus. Reprinted by permission of Hill and Wang, a division of Farrar, Strauss & Giroux, Inc. and by permission of Heinemann Publishers (Oxford), Ltd., for world rights.

9

Imperialism

And softly, as a hill survives,
resisting the weight of grass, wind, sunstroke,
as birds compose
voluntaries in air
after a yolked, hard beginning,
we rehearse
their acts of endurance,
we perform
their freedom,
making confession:
    in the violence of our coming
    this place has possessed us
    this place has possessed us
    all who came
    victor and victim
    its possession.

Dennis Scott, "All Saints," *Uncle Time.*[1]

The concept of imperialism is the single most weighty piece of intellectual baggage that students bring into the classes I teach. For them, imperialism is the illegitimate use and abuse of power by Europeans, especially British, to exploit and dominate the rest of the world. Their understanding is often circular: imperial domination is the thing to be explained, but imperialism is the explanation. The concept comprises not only the conquest and rule of colonies but indeed all contact, all trade, all cultural influence, even the spread of diseases. In the minds of many students, all of these processes are governed by European aggression and abuse of their superior power. When they understand imperialism, what is there left for me to teach, besides information to document their beliefs?

As usual, in my perversity, I do not understand imperialism but I want to. I cannot take the advice W. K. Hancock gave over forty years ago simply to get rid of the word as an obstacle to understanding. Hancock believed that the word's pejorative connotations and its use in political mudslinging left it with no analytical value at all. Yet it will not go away; I will have to deal with it. And this tension between its analytical meanings and its status as a term of abuse is one of the things I want to discuss with students.

The concept, at least implicitly, runs through all these pages. The purpose of this chapter, briefly, is to single out a few ways to overcome preconceived student attitudes, so that discussion can proceed. My hope is to persuade some of the students, whose minds are so firmly made up, to reopen to a tentative and analytical consideration of the relationships between Europeans and the people they contact around the world in modern times.

I am not a student of those early twentieth-century theories of Lenin, Hilferding, Rosa Luxemburg, or Karl Kautsky. Their writings are, to me, a branch of European intellectual history, and I have never found these debates very interesting or helpful in understanding imperial history. I look for imperialism at the point of contact between Europeans and Africans or Asians. I want to see what is going on at the quai side, as merchants barter. I want to eavesdrop as the missionary Hope Waddell converses with King Eyo Honesty in Calabar in the 1850s. When the British and the Asante kingdom go to war, I want to examine both sides.

But it will not do only to submerge myself into narratives of specific events. The question of the nature of imperialism is a question of the meaning and nature of detailed events such as these and of the very purpose of narrating them.

To get around existing preconceptions, I engage in an ongoing set of classroom exercises. If any set of activities, ideas, or processes is defined as imperialism, then a corresponding set of activities, ideas, or processes is *not imperialism*. Asking what is not imperialism proves to be a fruitful way to learn what imperialism is. More often, defining the not-imperialism exposes weaknesses in whatever current definition of imperialism we are discussing. I invite students to think up not-imperialisms for themselves.

One promising not-imperialism is a state of equality of power in the relations between two peoples contacting one another. Students commonly assume that Europeans had overwhelming advantages of power in nearly all contact situations from the fifteenth century onwards. It is useful to examine individual cases of contact to see what are the power relations at a given place and time— European ships at the Isle of Pines in the 1840s, or whatever other case we can find.

Beyond detailed individual cases, we can construct some broad generalizations: that Europeans were weaker than other Old World societies at the point of contact until the end of the fifteenth century; on a par, and gaining, with those societies in the sixteenth and seventeenth; pulling away in the eighteenth, so that by the late nineteenth century, and only then, the most technologically advanced European states could present overwhelmingly superior power at local points around the world without even much effort. These are broad and tentative generalizations, but they are concrete and testable, and their purpose is to seek out and explain anomalies— Cortez' victory in the early sixteenth century (in the New World, to be sure), and Cetshwayo's victory at Isandhlwana in 1879.

Another not-imperialism worth considering is free trade. The assumption here is that the imperialism consists of the coercive elements in the economic exchanges between European and Asian or African traders. Free trade doctrine is founded on the theory of comparative advantage and the conviction that economic exchange is mutually advantageous.

Free trade as an alternative to imperialism is an old idea. The old British empire had been based on mercantilism. Historians writing between the wars believed the triumph of free trade in mid-nineteenth-century Britain had ushered in a generation of anti-imperialism. They cited her devolution of authority from existing colonies and the official reluctance to acquire more.

In their pathbreaking 1953 article, Ronald Robinson and John Gallagher popularized the idea of a "free trade imperialism." They cited Britain's steady expansion throughout the midcentury decades and the frequent use of force to open up markets and make trade 'free.' They noted, too, that superior communications, organization and market knowledge and the instability of markets for primary products might give the Europeans systematic advantages in the seemingly equal exchange of free trade.

In my class, it will not do simply to accept the Robinson and Gallagher view of things. We need at least to inquire rather than presuming to know the answer in advance. Even in today's world, I note, free trade is widely viewed as not-imperialism. Whenever a trading nation has too much success, we will hear the accusation that that nation must be resorting to bounties, dumping, or reserved markets. When there are real imbalances and winners and losers in international trade, we begin to suspect that imperialism is at work.

A different aspect of imperialism is invoked when we pose nationalism as the not-imperialism. An empire is a multiethnic state, the nation a single ethnicity claiming the rights of self-determination. Whether in the nineteenth-century Hapsburg realms or twentieth-century Africa, nationalism was the major challenge to imperial rule. Ostensibly, one represented tyranny, the other freedom. No student doubts which was which. I offer instead a confrontation between imperial order and a prospect of nationalist anarchy, which could render freedom meaningless. This is not done to justify colonial rule but rather to foster a critical examination of the nature of imperialism—and of nationalism for that matter. I examine this idea further in chapter 13.

Another not-imperialism, apparently, is benign power. My students are divided about this but a large bloc claims that the United States wields its power benignly rather than selfishly, unlike other historic empires, such as the Soviet or the British. Fortunately, settlement of this question does not come within the subject matter of any course I teach. I do point out that the *claim* of benign power, of "we want nothing for ourselves," was an important feature of the ideological support of those other empires too. Over and over in British imperial history, for example, conquests were justified in a rhetoric of British duty, service, and sacrifice in providing the benefits of order and progress to those being conquered.

Again, as American history was taught for many decades, pioneer settlement and westward expansion were both not-imperialism. The standard term for these processes was rather manifest destiny. In *Doctrines of Imperialism*, A. P. Thornton invokes the classic distinction between overseas and overland expansion:

> . . . the process of *overland* expansion has been awarded
> an acceptance and favor of a kind denied to the spec-
> tacular, far-flung depredations of the sea powers, fanning

out from continental beachheads and bridgeheads to which they had clearly no 'right' in the first place. Climbing a range of hills or crossing a river in order to command the farther horizon seem natural, almost involuntary acts: but taking ship has always been an adventure, a conscious act of will, one that expects to impinge on someone else's world, to pass within someone else's horizon. (p. 10)

But Thornton is writing ironically, and his tone serves to subvert the distinction, in my reading of the passage. This view of overland expansion as not-imperialism was made possible, really, by the isolation of American from other historiographies and the firm civic agenda of American textbooks. As Native American history has come to be more fully incorporated into the story, this not-imperialism has been redefined, more and more, as a species of imperialism.

The not-imperialism implicit in my students' preconceived theory of imperialism has, in fact, sharply contrasting implications. This not-imperialism is isolation, the idea that the contact of Europe with other world regions should never have happened. In student notions, imperialism is all European expansion around the world—not only all the conquests and settlements, but all contact, all trade, all cultural influence, all environmental and epidemiological impact. This is the sentimental, Columbus-should-have-stayed-at-home school of thought, and it is very common, with many people eschewing any 'celebration' of the five hundredth anniversary of Columbus' voyage.

This is the most troublesome and unwieldy of the not-imperialisms for discussion. I argue with students that this tacit definition of imperialism is too sweeping and all-inclusive to have analytical value. Here is an enormous counterfactual rewriting of all of modern history. The purpose of my courses is to explain the world we have. To assume the enduring isolation of peoples from each other posits an entirely different world. We cannot really imagine what such a world would be like, but the very existence of any of us as individuals surely depends on the world we have. And our very sensibilities, including our disapprovals of imperialism, racism, and ethnocentrism, are things we only could have learned through experiencing the often terrible realities of modern world history.

When all is said and done, however, imperialism is not an adequate vehicle for analyzing the interaction between Europe and the wider world in modern times. Even playing with the various not-imperialisms will not take the place of analyzing historical data more closely. I suspect that imperialism could be a more useful concept than some of its theorists make it out to be. Too often, they try to create all-encompassing theories to explain everything. Such theories are always vulnerable to criticism, and the debate is endless.

I prefer, most of the time, to take some smaller, less ambitious stabs at the historical reality we are trying to understand. These are attempts not to explain everything, but something, or several somethings, and to see what these attempts would add up to. These are the installments of Gandhian truth I have been talking about, and I can mention a few more here, which pertain directly to the interpretation of imperialism. Whether they could be synthesized, finally, into a new general concept of imperialism I somewhat doubt.

When I pursue these approaches, some students may suspect me of merely seeking to replace the term with euphemisms. What I want to do, rather, is to separate out different processes, measure their impact, and place them back into the broader context.

I take, first, the evolving disease environment. Not a few students have extended one anecdote about smallpox blankets in the American West into a worldwide, half-millennium genocidal attack by Europeans on all other peoples. Any epidemic, they assume, must have been perpetrated on purpose. This is simply ignorance. A survey of epidemiological exchanges and of the history of plagues and peoples gives students an explanatory tool they can then use to enrich their understanding of whatever case they are studying.

Again, I present the histories of trade in various commodities, as these move from local and regional to global exchanges of increasing bulk, value, and complexity. Furs, gold and silver, sugar, tea, cotton, tobacco—these and others eventually form a complex network that grows to encompass the world, connecting all regions and all continents.

The related great demographic shifts, the movements of Europeans, Africans, Indians, and Chinese in modern times (and the displacement of indigenous peoples on several continents to make way for these immigrants,) to supply labor for producing and processing these commodities, encompass some of the truly horrible realities of modern history. And these population movements give us the world we have, though this should not be a statement made to dismiss student concerns. Students being really quite emotionally upset by these episodes is a reality of the classroom and one I do not have an easy time dealing with.

When we come to studying the imperialist scramble for territory of the nineteenth century, it is sometimes interesting to turn things around and study the foreign policy of those on the receiving end of the European advance. Imperialism, as traditionally studied, is heavily Euro-centric. What are the goals and options of an African or Pacific ruler facing possible takeover by one or another European powers? Imperialism looks a little different from this standpoint. Thus I consider the case of King Khama of the Ngwato people of Botswana, who played the Boer republics, Cecil Rhodes' chartered company, the Cape Colony, missionary societies, and the British Government against each other to protect the interests of his people even as they were annexed into the British imperial system.

By Khama's time, as noted above, Europeans' advantages in technology and communications, developed over centuries, had become overwhelming. Khama's state existed under the umbrella of British imperial hegemony. I suspect Khama understood this. Yet to note only British dominance and fail to describe Khama's brilliant statesmanship would create a thin and inadequate account of how the imperialist process worked in practice.

Another exercise in looking at imperialist annexation from below comes from New Zealand history. I distribute to students copies of the Treaty of Waitangi of 1840. The class becomes the Maori chiefs considering the treaty, I, the British consul urging them to sign. We scrutinize the text, noting discrepancies between the English version and a literal translation of the Maori text. Students are usually inclined to make too much of these. We discuss the historical situation thoroughly. I quote Tamati Waka Nene's statement that only the shadow of the land will pass to the Queen while the substance remains with the Maori people.

Most classes refuse to sign—but the Maoris gathered at Waitangi in 1840 did sign! As the discussion continues, I point out the hindsight bias by which the class takes into account all the later history of western imperialism, realities the Maoris of 1840 could not possibly have been aware of. And beyond this, I point out the tendency of the class to assume a paternalist and imperialist view that the Maoris at Waitangi were 'innocent natives' being duped and fooled. And such deprecation is off the mark! The actual debate the Maoris carried out in 1840 hinged on the implications of the treaty for their land, culture, and autonomy; they showed, in short, a pretty full awareness of what was at stake.

This discussion of the Treaty of Waitangi does not yield a single correct interpretation, and that is not what I was aiming at. At the beginning, perhaps, students found judging the episode easy, straightforward, and automatic. My goal was to make it more difficult.

These are cases involving the expansion of empire, annexation, and takeovers. For the imperialism of colonial rule itself, I refer back to the "colonizer and colonized" and other models for studying societies under colonial rule dealt with at length in chapter 5.

None of these approaches whitewashes or dismisses imperialism, and none simply attempts to attack and destroy student preconceptions. Each of the approaches is partial and tentative, and each aims to test a small segment of evidence against larger theories. Students usually, in fact, remain convinced of the systematic oppression of Third World societies by European power, consistently over five hundred years, through an evil process called imperialism. If a telling case is to be made for this proposition, I will argue, then some combination of the approaches I have outlined above will prove to be the best way to make it.

I still find it unlikely that history will yield such unambiguous moral lessons. In the passage quoted at the beginning of this chapter, the Jamaican poet Dennis Scott catches some of the double-edged irony in New World history. Even from the point of view of the victims of imperialism, he implies, the experience of modern history has been rich and creative as well as hard and brutal.

NOTE

1. These lines from the poem "All Saints" are reprinted from *Uncle Time*, by Dennis Scott, by permission of the University of Pittsburgh Press. ©1973 by Dennis Scott.

10

Nationalism and Racism: The Keywords

It is by words and the defeat of words,
Down sudden vistas of the vain attempt,
That for a flying moment one may see
By what cross-purposes the world is dreamt.

Richard Wilbur, "An Event," *Things of This World*.

For an hour and a half two men argued. They were vehement
and sometimes raised their voices, but there was no sense of personal
hostility. In the end they still disagreed. They even disagreed about
whether some slight movement on someone's part was a possible
outcome. I could not get the floor during this discussion, and I am
not sure what I would have contributed if I had. I sympathized with
the ideal that persuasion was the purpose of argument, but I feared
that whole areas of fundamental disagreement remained unexplored.
The failure of the discussion, I decided later, was not the failure
of one to persuade the other but the failure to clarify what the
disagreement was about. Though the individual positions were stated
with eloquence, the combination was baffingly uncoordinated. The
two men were talking past each other, speaking different languages.
When the very terminology of the discussion is not mutually
understood, persuasion is doubly difficult. Nor am I optimistic about
my own ability to define the issues to the satisfaction of the
antagonists, or of either of them. All I can hope for is to improve
my own understanding of the issues they were raising. And since
the deepest misunderstandings seemed to come from the use of
language, it is to language that I will turn.

1. Words and World

The keywords of the discussion were *nationalism* and *racism*. Such words are, first of all, generalizations which summarize entire categories of social phenomena. By using these words, seemingly, the speaker can shortcut paragraphs of explanation and invoke the entire category straightaway. On the simplest level, the problem is that the images intended by the speaker are not the same as those raised in the listener's mind. In other words, they disagree about the meanings of the terms, though they might not realize right away what the problem is.

At a slightly more complex level, speaker, listener, or both might forget that the conceptual term—say, *nationalism*—is a generalization and not the reality itself. Disagreements about the nature of nationalist movements in history then degenerate into arguments about the meaning of the term *nationalism*. The social phenomena and the shortcut terms are confused for one another. People speak as if a concept—the word *nationalism*—is a fact or an object existing in the world.

These types of confusion occur frequently in the usage of *nationalism* and *racism*, but just to clear these away does not yet provide the clarification I am seeking. There are still deeper levels of misunderstanding beyond these. One of these, it seems to me, is the frequent confusion between disagreements based on values and disagreements of fact or evidence. One historical account of a nationalist movement might be sympathetic and favorable, another hostile and dismissive; yet they might use exactly the same sources, cite the same evidence, convey identical historical information. It is simply that one account values the movement while the other condemns it. The difference between them rests in values, not facts. As I have posed the case, the basis of disagreement would be easy to see, but in reality, two accounts never use exactly the same data. Historical accounts are always selective, and there are endless variations of context in which a given historical incident might be placed. Disagreements of value are therefore always deeply enmeshed within disagreements about evidence. The difference in values between two accounts means that the available facts are placed in different orders of subordination and significance, until the basis of disagreement is often very difficult to see clearly.

We are getting closer, I hope, to understanding how an argument about *nationalism* and *racism* can become muddled, but there are deeper levels yet to explore.

Nationalism and *racism* are words. The problems they raise as words are more than their ambiguity, more than the need to distinguish between concept and social phenomenon, more than the confusion in historical accounts between statements of value and statements of fact. As words, these terms have a historical development of their own quite apart from the social realities they symbolize. The problems of fact and value occur not only in accounts of individual nationalist movements but also in the treatment of *nationalism* as a word or an idea. One individual might be favorable to nationalism and want his people to share his feelings; another might oppose nationalist sentiment as false consciousness. The history of the word and the reputation of the idea are cases of shifting denotation and shifting connotation—changes in the kinds of facts represented by the word and in the kinds of values implied in the word. An exploration of some of these shifts of meaning will, I hope, finally get us to a level of understanding in which we can see the difficulties the two debaters were having, even beyond what the two men themselves fully perceived.

In this discussion I will rule out of order and will not consider any and all uses of the word *nation* and its derivatives that pertain to the sovereign state. These uses of the word have their own standing, but they beg the question of the relationships between nation and state that I would want to analyze. For present purposes, the nation is only the group of people and not their state. Also, though I have so far considered mainly *nationalism*, I will in what follows also consider *racism* with a parallel and related treatment.

2. Connotations

Nation and *race* are closely related in past usage. In the nineteenth and early twentieth centuries they were nearly interchangeable. The "race question" in Canada or South Africa, for example, referred to conflicts between British and French or British and Afrikaners. It was not quite simply a loose usage of *race* to mean what we mean by *nation*. It was that nations were thought to have a racial basis. A nation was defined as a historically differentiated group, with elements of common history, language, customs, and

traditions, possessing or aspiring to its own state. In the theory of
the time each nation claimed an eternal existence, and the explanation for its distinctiveness was racial. With the prevalence of ideas
about the inheritance of acquired characteristics, each nation was
thought to have a particular genius, biologically inherited by the
common racial stock making up the group. *Nation* was interchangeable with *race* as a designation for the group because the group was
racial in its formation. With the twentieth-century decline of
Lamarckian theories of biological-cultural inheritance, the two
concepts of *race* and *nation* moved apart. But more than a trace
of these assumptions of a special genius, often incommunicable and
incomprehensible to outsiders, survives in many nationalist ideologies.

By the late twentieth century, the two words have become
markedly distinct in meaning and in their 'ism' form even more
distinct in value. *Nation* denotes the ethnic group in possession of
or striving for its own state. *Nationalism* is the ideology of
commitment to the strivings of the nation or loyalty to its state. With
the popularity of self-determination and of the rights of self-
government in the anti-colonial revolt, *nationalism* came to possess
sharply positive value connotations (with exceptions to be noted
later). *Racism*, on the other hand, acquired strongly negative
connotations, since the day when Lord Milner could proudly term
himself a "British Race Patriot." The very defining of racial groups
came to seem suspect, especially when used as a basis for enforcing
other kinds of social distinctions. *Racism* has retained its association
with stereotyped group characteristics and of cultural affinities
acquired by inheritance, but the term is narrowed in its application
to groups defined by specific physical characteristics, especially skin
color. It should be clear, however, that *race* for racists is in fact not
biologically but rather socially defined; for them, racism forms an
ideological justification for group inequality, persecution, or even
genocide (see sections 5 and 6 in this chapter).

Racism and *nationalism* have moved as far apart as possible
in their reputations: the one term connoting positive values of
patriotism and liberty, the other negative values of oppression and
injustice. But this sharp contrast of meaning is really in connotation,
in the values placed on the terms. How distinct the terms are in
denotation, if we could strip the connotations away, remains for
us to examine.

But stripping away the connotations from these words is a difficult, some might say impossible, exercise. For the doubters, perhaps, the connotations *are* the words' meanings. For others the words represent an aspect of reality in the world and cannot be separated in their minds from that reality. But the exercise I am attempting seems to me valuable, even necessary. As we have seen, when the speaker's use of a term invokes in the hearer a different value or a different reality from the one intended, then communication fails. The examination of the terms stripped of their connotations, however artificially, is the only way I can think of to pinpoint and illuminate this failure of communication.

The misunderstanding between speaker and listener is not caused, first of all, by one of them being *wrong* about the words' definitions. Words mean what people decide they mean. Whether *nationalism* and *racism* have positive or negative connotations is arbitrary and subject to change. And the existence of races or nations is not a fixed fact but really a socially determined, conventional way of interpreting the world. The acceptance of such an interpretation is, of course, itself a historical event occurring at a particular time. It is not a permanent truth. People can disagree and even try to change these meanings and the interpretations based on them.

3. Analysis of the Nationalist Movement

Ernest Gellner shows convincingly, I think, that the nation does not exist for all time but only when a nationalist comes to believe in its existence. In what follows I draw heavily on his work but adapt freely.

To begin with, the nationalist must discern and define the common features of a population group which make it, to him, a nation. This nation, he argues, has a common past and therefore should have a common destiny in the form of its own independent state. Two or more people sharing these beliefs, striving for their realization, would be a nationalist movement. They would have two tasks. One would be to convince as many as possible of the members of the defined catchment group that they are all members of the nation and that all the injustices and inadequacies of their lives would be overcome by membership in and commitment to it. In other words, the movement's first task is to raise the nationalist consciousness of the defined group.

The second task of the movement would be to establish and gain recognition for its state in its territory. This involves sweeping aside the existing sovereign of the territory (the empire?) and defeating any rival nationalist claims to the territory or to political authority.

Gellner relates such movements to modern changes in production, communications, education, and occupational recruitment. In this way he fixes nationalism to a certain point in human history. That is how he demonstrates that the nation does not exist from time eternal—even though it is a central part of many nationalist ideologies to claim such eternal existence.

The catchment, the potential members of the nation, have to be *defined*. Taking only the common criteria of nationalism, the number of potential nations is beyond counting. Of possible nations, only a small number find any adherents, and only a few of these succeed in their goals. It is only success that establishes legitimacy. We tend to forget this, accepting the nationalist premise that the nation is permanent with a right to its own state as simply the natural order of things. We consider reality from the point of view of successful nations; they alone are worthy of consideration. The positive value connotation of *nationalism* is the judgment of the victors. I will return later to the (terminological) fate of unsuccessful movements.

From this brief account we can single out a number of victims or enemies of the nationalist movement:

a. People loyal to the empire or other existing territorial government.

b. Nationalists who want to recruit part of the catchment into another nation.

c. Nationalists who want to govern the territory in the name of another nation.

d. People in the catchment who do *not* accept the premise that the nation will remedy the injustices they suffer and who perhaps opt for some other kind of movement to do this. (To the nationalists, such people are traitors; it may be necessary for the nation to force them to be free.)

e. Residents of the territory who are not in the catchment group. (The nation can deal with these people by assimilation, extermination, expulsion, or toleration in a subordinate status.)

This is a formidable list of enemies and victims. In fact, the great extent to which nationalism seems a positive and legitimate force is surprising—but victims do not always get a good press. The acceptance of the nationalist premise as 'natural' is one of the distinctive features of the last century and a half. We note here, too, that some of the enemies of the nationalist movement are other nationalists. What then?

4. Judgments of Nationalism

Nationalism is a group loyalty. The existence of the sentiment, I have argued, is what brings the group into existence. We have seen, also, that the types of groups that can be defined as nations are numerous, with only success establishing legitimacy. There is therefore an interesting tendency to downgrade unsuccessful groups, calling them by lesser names. An African group loyalty with all of the classic linguistic, historical, and cultural ingredients of nationalism will be called *tribalism* if it does not fit the imposed state boundaries. Violence by such a group in pursuit of its goals is termed *tribal warfare*, a judgment that it is not about anything worthwhile. Similarly, in South Asia before 1947, religious based group loyalties were called *communalism* (loyalty to the religious community), an illegitimate, divisive force which threatened imperial and national efforts to transfer power to a united subcontinental government. (In the end, of course, partition made Islamic nationalism all right for Pakistan.) But *within* state boundaries, communalism was still considered divisive, backward looking, and destructive, so that, though identical in content with nationalism, it was not given that honorific name.

Such judgments are judgments of the victors. The real fault of communal or tribal movements is failure. They seem backward looking and unprogressive, but is not this also true of many nationalisms, if we can but ignore the positive veneer that overlays the inner content? Human beings define their groups in two ways. They first of all invoke and celebrate the common characteristics and virtues of the group. They also, and this is universal, create disparaging stereotypes of their rivals and neighbors, and this process helps define the virtues of the group by expressing what the group is not. Group loyalty is then an expression of particularistic values and perforce a denial of universal humanistic ones: part of the process is to exaggerate the differences between peoples and to establish and maintain boundaries. And to dehumanize enemies, rivals, or outgroups helps justify the struggle against them.

It may be that without this negative process the group would not define itself as a group. There is no 'us' without a contrasting 'them.' Group identity is brought about only by the existence of outlanders, groups that the given group is apart from. The struggle against these others, who may be oppressors, victims, or just neighbors, helps the nationalist movement recruit and unify the people of the catchment. Customs of the group are maintained partly by stressing how outlandish are the customs of others. I would argue, therefore, that a feeling of superiority to and disparagement of 'others' is a universal characteristic of nationalism, though its virulence may vary widely. Certainly, all peoples appear to have a vocabulary for belittling others.

When analysis of these elements is combined with the history of intergroup relations, of domination, subordination, territorial rivalry, dispossession, and massacre, then all of the history of nationalist conflict in European history can be readily imagined.

The victims and enemies of nationalism have not, of course, been entirely silent. This negative side of nationalism is emphasized in a good deal of writing in which nationalism is blamed for the anarchy of modern Europe. Some writing in this vein goes further, condemning even the positive side, the evocation of the traditions and characteristics of the group as a means of group pride. In such writing, much but not all of it Marxist, the trend of history moves away from particularities of culture toward a general and common culture of shared values. Nationalist loyalties, in this view of history, are seen as backward survivals, atavisms, or obstacles to a progressive humanism, no different from what is termed *tribalism* or *communalism* in Africa or Asia. Such writing can and often does go beyond the descriptive historical account (here is the historical trend) over to a prescriptive program (here is what ought to happen to make the world a better place.)

I said at the very beginning I only hoped to understand the issues of nation and race better myself. And with nationalism that is perhaps all I have accomplished. My analysis looks at nationalism from the outside. The nationalist thinks about these issues from the inside, and nationalism for a committed adherent can provide a total moral universe. This kind of commitment may preclude his understanding my discussion, and he could even see it as an attack.

All I can do about this is to assess the difference between his vision and mine. My assumption is that nations are one type of human group loyalty, which I analyze in a 'uniformitarian' way; for him one nation is unique and morally privileged. I wish to raise general hypotheses that could be tested in the case of any nation; he will say that outsiders do not understand and cannot make valid statements about his nation. From my outside view, I believe that nationalism has transformed the tradition on which it is based by making it into a politically conscious ideology; from his inside view, he believes that his nationalism *is* the tradition. My consideration of nationalism is intellectual; his experience of nationalism is affective.

I cannot bridge this gap, but I must insist that my analysis is not an attack on the nation. I am not saying that all nations are exactly alike. I will ask the same questions about each nation, but I do not expect to get the same answers. I mean a given nation no harm, therefore, when I place it in the same context as the notorious other for purposes of comparison. And should I speak of the nation as a contingent and possibly ephemeral type of human organization, I am only trying to define words and am not contemplating the destruction of peoples. Similarly, should I compare two cases of nationalist behavior, I am only trying to explain events and am not accusing a given people of heinous crimes.

5. Racism and Nationalism

It seems more difficult to manipulate the values or connotations of *racism* in the manner I have attempted with *nationalism*. The term is so firmly pejorative, so fixed as a doctrine of injustice, oppression, disparagement, and hatred, that I simply risk misunderstanding in attempting such an exercise. While the negative side of *nationalism* is at least familiar and easy to see in operation, how could we imagine a positive racism? Yet consider the following: If nationalism is belief in the cause of a nation, racism *could* be defined as belief in the cause of a race. The term *could* be used to designate pride in a group defined by race. I do not, of course, desire or expect the word to be so redefined.

My point here is that there is a problem with the terminology for racially based group identities and loyalties. The close relationship between these and nationalism is obvious, especially since most nationalisms did, or do, claim common ancestry or a limited gene pool as one source of the group's existence. And in European colonial empires, where racist oppression supported imperial domination, racially based nationalist group identities were widespread. Looked at in this way, racially defined group loyalties are simply a variant of nationalism, no more arbitrary or exclusivist than any other. But they are racially based, and in a variety of settings *they are called racist*.

Such groups are, in other words, condemned out of hand. There is great irony in the act of condemning the victims of racist oppression as racist themselves as soon as they assert their identity and pride. But it is true that racially exclusive groups deny the universalist criteria of liberal and modern society—as do all nationalist movements to some degree. The habit of disparaging or hating outgroups, for racially based groups, could well take the form of racism in its usual sense, but is it for all that necessarily more unpleasant or vicious than nationalist xenophobias have been, with their linguistic or religious prejudice?

What I am trying to suggest is that our definitions of words, with their strong value connotations, get us tangled up in our attempts to understand reality. By placing positive values on the term *nationalism* we seem to say that nations are a more appropriate and natural form of human loyalty; at the same time, the strongly negative connotations of the term *racism* spill over and seem to imply that any and all cases of racial group definition must be based on the virulent hatred of others. A group defined by race may well emphasize pride in the positive characteristics of the group itself as a means of overcoming past injustice and oppression. Both nations and group loyalties based on race, I would argue, can be judged positively and negatively—liberationist and positive racial loyalties as well as ugly hatred of other racial groups; oppressive and xenophobic nationalism as well as liberating national selfdetermination. All of these types are possible, and in a morally complex world may sometimes form Jekyll and Hyde aspects of the same movements.

6. Social Race

The great variation within the human species brought about by the long-term isolation of gene pools is the fact of biological race. That some of the observable physical differences are singled out in a society as marks of group membership is the fact of social race.

Thus, biological race and social race are not the same thing. The way physical differences are perceived and used to create social groupings is capricious and arbitrary, different for every society that makes such distinctions. It is impossible to assign every member of society rigorously to a racial group based on biological race, most simply, because rigorously distinct biological races do not exist. Each society making such distinctions has to create customs and rules for doing so. Race is not, any more than nation, a 'natural' or inevitable basis for human groups. In the past, as we have seen from the account of nationalism, racial designations have always been entangled in cultural ones. Culture was regarded as racially determined, and even recent racism, as in South Africa under Apartheid, still made this connection.

One strand of the opposition to racism has been an attempt to eliminate race as a social category. It is from this perspective, sometimes, that oppressed racial groups asserting their group pride have been criticized. If racial distinctions are a vehicle of oppression, it is argued, the best way to overcome the oppression is to do away with the group definition altogether. This is good liberalism, but it has not worked that way historically. Unilaterally imposed racial grouping does occur, but even groups created by the fiat of the oppressors have asserted themselves positively, using their solidarity as a means of identity and pride. As we have seen, this assertion is quite likely to be criticized as racist or condemned as illiberal.

Such criticisms seem to imply, first, that racial group identities are less valid than national ones. But we have seen that either type of group is arbitrarily defined by society. The important distinctions should be between voluntary and imposed groups and between liberating and oppressive ones.

Critics of racial pride movements also assert that the groups' opposition to oppression by the invoking of racial identity is a second-best response. The racial movement in this view is trapped in a false consciousness, which accepts the criteria of the oppressor and misses the class definitions by which the most effective allies can be won, the most effective goals reached, with less danger of turning liberation into another oppression. This is the same Marxist criticism that viewed nationalist loyalties as obstacles to progressive development. Still another criticism of positive racial loyalties is that the oppressed group, in the very act of its group assertion, repeats inevitably the error of hating or at least disparaging the outgroup.

All do this; it is universal among nationalists and seems inescapable however the groups are defined. But that is only to propose that human beings should not define themselves into any groups smaller than humanity as a whole. We cannot hope to eliminate conflict in human society. There will be groups. We can only hope to mitigate the worst excesses.

By and large, liberal or Marxist attempts to bypass or abolish particularist group identities have failed. The social and economic forces that they expected would dissolve away the particularities were, ironically, the very forces that led to the rise of modern nationalism. The universalist ideologies have had to compromise with the particularist group loyalties, establishing themselves, at best, underneath the aegis of nationalist states, where they could hope to foster the positive side of nationalist group loyalty. Certainly, too, proponents of these allegedly universalist beliefs, however high their ideals, are themselves riddled with exlusivist sectarian divisions. But that is another topic. It is enough to repeat here that nationalist-type loyalties also have their positive content, and that if such loyalties are the occasion and the symbol, they are not necessarily the root cause of man's many inhumanities to man.

7. The Argument Between Two Men

I may seem to have forgotten the argument between two men. I have not referred directly to what they said, But I believe I have explored and encompassed the ways in which they misunderstood each other. The overlapping and ambiguous meanings of *nationalism* and *racism* became entangled one with another. The denotation of a word became entangled with its connotation. An attitude toward a concept was confused with a judgment about a reality existing in the world. Affect vehemently confronted analysis.

In more specific terms, criticisms of the policy of a state were mistaken for denigration of an entire people, because the same word, the name of the nationalism, was used in different senses. Further, an ideological hostility to *nationalism* as an unprogressive force was taken for an implicit threat to the existence of the adherents of a particular nationalism.

At the roots of the entire controversy, the calling of a given nationalism by the term *racism* was provocatively insulting to the believers in that nationalism, especially since they had been victims of oppression as a 'race'. The argument was, whatever else, a breakdown in terminology. To state that elements of a nationalism might be exclusivist, that these elements might disparage outsiders, stereotype them, and, sufficiently threatened by conflict, persecute them, is only to say that the movement is nationalist.

My feeling that I learned a lot from the discussion is tempered by a suspicion that I could not convey my understanding to either of the men arguing so vociferously that afternoon.

11

Structures of Argument in African History

                                    . . . I
          flung open long-disused windows
          and doors and saw my hut
          new-swept by rainbow brooms
          of sunlight become my home again
          on whose trysting floor waited
          my proud vibrant life.

Chinua Achebe, "Answer," *Christmas in Biafra and Other Poems.*[1]

In the middle 1950s, when I was still an undergraduate, African history was just being born. We had one book, K. Onwuke Dike's *Trade and Politics on the Niger Delta*. African history would be more books like this. For more information, we had to read Samuel Johnson's *History of the Yoruba,* or other books of that type— pioneering works of history written by Africans who were amateur historians trying to reconstruct the past of their peoples; or such works as Sir Alan Burns' *History of Nigeria*, colonial-centered works by colonial administrators.

Thirty-five years later it is difficult to imagine that the academic beginnings are so recent. Today there are dozens of journals, hundreds of monographs on every imaginable subject, with more coming monthly. There is a plenitude of detailed and sophisticated textbooks, and even grand syntheses in at least two versions—the UNESCO History of Africa and the Cambridge History of Africa, both coming out in multi-volumed sets.

African history had to fight for its status. "Africa has no history," it was confidently asserted. Africans had never accomplished anything. This was part of a larger racist disparagement of Africa and her people, and a good deal of African history was written quite explicitly as an answer to these attacks. This gives some African history a little the tone of apologetics, in the sense that an attack has been made and the historian is answering this attack. Such answers were necessary and salutary but had the disadvantage that the attacker had framed the question to be answered. The historian accepts the terms of the attack—that the significance, value, and status of African history need defending, need establishing. The more scholarly and academic the work, of course, the less this quality is evident. But hints of apologia can nevertheless still be discerned in even the dryest of monographs, if only in topic selection and in the introductions.

The birth of academic African history was simultaneous with the moving of the African colonies of European powers to independent nationhood. This is no coincidence. African history was in the service of the new nations. It would be an important part of the curriculum of schools and new universities, institutions that would educate a national citizenry and train men and women for government service. The struggle to establish the significance of African history is parallel with the struggle to establish, maintain, and develop the independence of the new African nations.

For this reason, perhaps, a good deal of African history has a presentist quality. Maybe this is no more true than in other fields of history, but it seems so to me. Current problems and priorities did a good deal to dictate the kinds of topics historians would work on. The first decade of independence saw nation-building as a key historical concern, followed by pan-African unity movements and a related historical search for common Africanness. When African nations, over the years, were plagued with problems of political instability, social unrest, the failure of economic growth, and, ultimately, economic dislocation, even famine, historical research followed along, looking for the historical roots and explanations of these problems.

Neither the apologetic nor the presentist agendas of African historical writing should be exaggerated. An enormous amount of African history has been written, an enormous amount of detailed information has been unearthed, written up, and synthesized. African history does exist. Any further attacks on its significance and status are surely by now merely ignorant and fatuous. It follows that, for some time now, the best strategy for those writing African history is to make no reference at all to these old racist attacks on the subject. It simply is no longer necessary to defend Africa and its history from this kind of attack.

Or almost not necessary. When I teach African history, I teach the subject straight, using the soberest and most matter-of-fact text and readings I can find. Many students find this approach unsatisfying. They are friends and defenders of African history, but to them, often, the apologias in defense of the subject are African history. Many of them are familiar with the works of Chancellor Williams, Cheikh Anta Diop, J. C. de Graft Johnson, or other works derived from these authors. They want to hear what Africans have achieved and how the racists have tried to deny these achievements. I am under suspicion myself, not least for the readings I assign. In many cases, students would rather read the most polemic amateur apologetics about Africa than the latest exciting (to me) synthesis of new research.

African history is hard for students to read and learn. The burden of unfamiliar names, places, and events is great. Pre-colonial histories are often highly technical in presenting how information is established. And, for the reasons outlined earlier, historiographical fashions have changed in rapid sequence.

Students, I have found, need a guide to the arguments being made by various authors. I found this out rather by accident. When students had read a given book, I would ask them for the argument. They did not realize there had been an argument. They believed that the author had told the story as it happened, that the structure of the book inhered in the actual events of history. This set me to the task of identifying the recurring structures of argument, as they evolved in the last three or four decades of African historical writing. I then can ask students to try to fit one or another of the models to the books they have read. The payoff of the exercise is that it fosters more active, less trusting reading habits on the part of the students. As I considered the various structures of argument, I worked out that it was the place given to Europeans in African history that was one key; the presence of one or another apologetic style, explicit or implied, was another.

What follows is my survey of the structures of argument in African history. I have not tied the various models to any particular works. I found that if I presented them as mere logical alternatives, they had a greater pedagogical impact. They could then be confirmed (or otherwise) by the students as they read in the literature.

African history is about the historical development of African societies, in the remote as well as the recent past. But however much scholars for the last generation have stressed the autonomy of African history, you never go for too long without considering the impact of Europe on African development. It of course remains an important element in half a millennium of African history. The emphasis on autonomy does not lead to the omission of the European factor; it rather creates a series of tensions between outside influence and internal development: imperialism and resistance, westernization and tradition, continuity and change, in constant interplay.

The simplest kind of argument about this interplay posits a three step process:

baseline → impact causing a transition → the result

Here, the baseline is a descriptive category—traditional, autonomous Africa. The middle element, impact, is the influence of the West, colonial rule, imperialism, the intrusion of modern life. The third element is contemporary Africa, the phenomenon to be explained, also a descriptive generalization. This general structure of argument can be seen in full form in numerous books about Africa and African history. Fragments of the argument sometimes serve to organize the detail in more specialized works. In addition, certain forms of the argument are present in journalism and in public statements about Africa. I will first outline four distinct variations on the general scheme shown above. I will then point out certain problems and shortcomings of the entire structure.

The three steps occur most often in two basic variations. The first assumes a positive baseline, through the transition, to a negative result. The second version simply reverses these values, from a negative baseline through the transition to a positive result:

1. free independent life → European exploitation → under-development
2. backwardness and disunity → colonial modernization → independent nations

These versions have in common the assumption of a decisive transition period; both assume that the Europeans did a great deal in and to Africa, whether constructively or destructively. Either model can be used to outline cultural, economic, or political changes. In the wording above, I have given variation #1 an economic tinge, variation #2 a political emphasis. These are perhaps the most common forms these two variations take. The difference between them is still mainly the reversal of values, one from positive to negative, the other from negative to positive.

Historians stressing the autonomy of African development tend to pare down and reduce the strength of the European impact. The middle element in the argument, imperialism, exploitation, colonial rule, becomes briefer, more superficial, with more free African agency operating even at its height. But the same three-fold scheme is still discernible, even with the assumed ineffectiveness of the impact:

3. backwardness, disunity → ineffective modernization → resurgence of disunity, weak and unstable regimes
4. free, independent life → cultural and economic imperialism → resurgence of free independent life

Both of these lines of reasoning assume the superficiality of the middle element, the European impact. Version #3, common in fragmentary form in American journalism, assumes that today's African instability is a throwback to traditional disunity ('tribal warfare,' 'ancient enmities'), which a brief and weak period of colonial rule was insufficient to erase. Version #4 is not only a historical interpretation but a political-cultural program for overcoming African problems today. In this version, past Africans had a just society based on egalitarian economic and social principles. European cultural imperialism and economic exploitation threatened this society, but were fortunately too weak and temporary to destroy the old ways utterly. The old customs were shaken but are still recoverable; *ujamaa* and *uhuru* can again be made the basis for just societies in Africa, despite the problems of instability, conflict, and inequality introduced during colonial rule—such is the ideological posture of a number of African regimes today.

Both these versions agree that colonial rule was brief and superficial—either too weak to do much good or too weak to do much harm (though harmful enough in most statements of this argument), and both versions regard today's African reality as a return to the precolonial past in important respects. Again, the one version is simply the other turned upside down.

As I have implied, in some statements of version #4 there is a thin line of contradiction running through the argument. This occurs when the destructive forces of imperialism or modern life are stressed so much that it seems that the populist past must be utterly destroyed; yet miraculously, though destroyed, it is available as the basis for building the new society.

This three step scheme in its variations is amazingly common, considering the grave problems that occur in its applications. Of these, the most serious is the difficulty in defining and describing the *baseline*. The three step scheme is reminiscent of that used in analyzing the impact of the industrial revolution on the workers' standard of living in eighteenth- and nineteenth-century England, and some of the same problems come up in that case. When did a baseline ever exist? The search for 'Africa untouched' at some past time *before* the impact of European contact assumes that African societies were locked in the stasis of their traditional life. This assumption is evident in the old idea that Africa was a primitive continent with no history but also exists in a different form, in descriptions of 'merrie Africa,' enjoying a free and independent life idealized as a golden age.

In trying to prove that Africa does have a history, again, some apologists make a sharp distinction between development and achievement by African agencies (praiseworthy, evidence of African capacity,) and African developments resulting from outside contact (illegitimate, deflecting Africa from natural lines of development.) The assumption here is that there is a definable Africanness that can be isolated. The task becomes a defining of this Africanness in its true, pristine form before any outside influence touched and tainted it. Not many writers go this far, but any attempt rigorously to define the baseline tends to move in this direction. A useful corrective would be to make African history an integral part of human history from the beginning. Africans were never totally isolated, and, furthermore, all the processes and relationships of contact existing between Africans and others also existed among Africans themselves. What is the difference?

The problem of defining the baseline is particularly evident in works which cover the time span from pre-colonial, through colonial rule, to independent Africa. The category *pre-colonial* cannot be dealt with adequately as a descriptive, generalized baseline, because pre-colonial African history has, in fact, great chronological depth. African societies were not static, and their histories can be recovered, in some cases, for more than two millennia into the past. And since African people were never isolated from other human developments, there is no such thing as "Africa untouched."

Attempts to describe this baseline 'Africa before the white man' also fall into two sharply contrasted variations. In the 'lost cities of Africa' approach, the emphasis is on African kingdoms, empires, and large scale territorial and bureaucratic states. With their Iron Age technology, these states can be seen as roughly equivalent to those of medieval Europe. I do not mean to question the value of a great deal of research in reconstructing the substantial histories of African kingdoms. I am only interested here in the emphasis on the 'lost cities' as it influences *argument* about African history.

The variant three-step processes examined previously can now be adapted to accommodate this emphasis on African political development. In variations #1 and #4, pre-colonial Africa was judged positively for its free, independent life. Pre-colonial African peoples were accomplishing something, which was either disrupted or carried on by Europeans before being resumed in contemporary independent Africa. In a variant application of the reasoning, one can argue not only that Africa has a history, but that the modern state of Ghana also does:

5. Opoku Ware, nation builder → Gov. Guggisberg, nation builder → Kwame Nkrumah, nation builder

In this version, all three stages are part of a single purposeful continuous development. The eighteenth-century king of Asante extending his domain, the twentieth-century British governor building roads and harbors, and the nationalist leader winning political independence are all doing the same thing.

A more common version applies the same reasoning but with a negative judgment of the colonial interlude, even of the best efforts of colonial rulers to prepare African territories for independence:

6. Traditional kingdom → Westminster model → *Uhuru* regime

This line of argument has been used to justify African departures from the constitutional arrangements left by colonial rule at the time

of the transfer of power. Even if based on a military coup, one man
rule or one party rule is judged to be a better expression of African
traditions than the alien Europeanstyle constitution had been.

In the contrasting view of precolonial society, the populist or
'African genius' version, the values placed on precolonial African
society are sharply altered. The greater the kingdoms and empires,
in this view, the greater the inequality and injustice being perpetrated.
There were large empires in the precolonial western Sudan, but they
were not African. They were rather slave-based conquest states
imposed by an external, alien imperialism, which interfered with
the popular democratic justice of African village life. This version
would be rendered something like this, as a refinement of the free
independent life scheme:

7. *ujamaa* society → colonial interlude → *ujamaa* society

This line of reasoning is, in fact, a version of Afro-phile apologetics in direct rivalry with the 'lost cities' version. Instead of
confronting European achievements in statescraft, science, and
technology with the assertion that Africans made these achievements
in equivalent fashion, this line rejects the significance of European
achievements. What is so great about great empires and armies,
compared to African justice and humanity?

> Heia for the reincarnation of tears and the worst pain
>   brought back again
> Those who never invented anything
> those who never tamed anything
>
> Heia for joy
> Heia for love. . .

(Aimé Césaire, *Return to My Native Land*, 76)[2]

Past racist disparagement of Africa and Africans often took the
form of distorted and unfair comparisons between Africa and Europe.
The European 'great community' of literacy, long-distance
commerce, church, and state (all of this equated with 'civilization')
would be compared with the African 'little community' of local
village life. The lost cities approach is one kind of answer to such
racist polemics—Africa has a great tradition too. This might be

termed the *apologetics of equivalence*. The African genius approach accepts the terms of the original comparison but overturns its values. The more large-scale politics, economics, and hierarchy in a society, this argument runs, the greater the injustices perpetrated on ordinary humanity. Africans are better-off for not having invented anything. This might be termed the *apologetics of difference*.

It is these perspectives, especially the apologetics of equivalence, that many students bring with them to class. But for them, as noted above, these positions are not apologetic but are the very truth of African history. One student, committed to the argument for equivalence, thought that Aime Cesaire's poem, "Return to My Native Land," was full of lies: "Those who never invented anything," indeed! I asked him why he thought Cesaire had taken such a position. Another student feared that if, as a book stated, Africa had borrowed certain techniques from the Ancient Near East, perhaps Africa was indeed deficient in creativity. I pointed out that the author's speculations, even if proven, would not warrant any such conclusion.

When I circulate documents portraying these apologetic positions, the class discussion does tread on delicate ground. If I say that the apologetics of equivalence and difference are defensive positions and ideological rationales (and of great interest as such,) I am right. But I am not thereby saying that they are altogether false in their implications for historical interpretation; nor am I thereby belittling or denying African cultural values or achievements. As stated elsewhere, a great deal of valuable historical work has come out of these orientations. Therefore, a student believing one of the positions to be 'true', is not wrong. But her truth, like mine, is a partial, Gandhian, installment and not the whole story.

The apologetics of difference and the apologetics of equivalence have a kind of economic counterpart. There is a long-term controversy between formalist interpretations of African society, in which the ordinary western economic theories are deemed suitable for the study of Africa and the contrasting substantivist line of argument in which the application of western categories of economic analysis is rejected. Market incentives, responsiveness to supply and demand, all of the ordinary facets of western economic behavior are found in Africa, in the formalist view. By contrast, substantivist scholars deny that western economic models can be applied to Africa. In their view, market values were not predominant. Rather, markets existed in society along with other, more important criteria for the distribution of resources: reciprocity and redistribution.

Starting from formalist assumptions, one could then argue that what western imperialism did was to deflect African development away from the possible indigenous economic revolution; whereas, starting from substantivist arguments, what western contact did was to distort African values toward the greed and inequality inherent in capitalist society, a society in which all else, human beings themselves not least, are subordinated to market demands.

The various sequences of African development outlined above are, pushed to their logical conclusion, incompatible with one another. Yet each has proved fruitful in stimulating lines of inquiry and opening up new vistas of African history. As we have seen, the differences between them are of two types: disagreements about facts and disagreements about values. Does the colonial experience represent development or destructive exploitation? Must the pre-colonial past be characterized as anarchic or as democratic? To go overboard for any one answer requires the selective use of evidence—facts are available to support any of these arguments. And two historians who agree that the European-sponsored transformation was decisive might disagree about whether this was a good or a bad thing. Here is the disagreement about value. Often, these disagreements of fact and value are combined and mixed together, much to the confusion of argument in African history.

As I have said, these approaches to African history have, whatever the incompatibilities between them, all been fruitful in developing research. But, as the colonial period recedes into the past, the veins of ore they reveal may be played out. The racist jibes about African history, even if still sometimes made, are finally and utterly discredited. In the future, I hope, African historians will no longer have to set their agenda through apologetic strategies to answer the old dismissive and racist distortions.

Despite the many efforts to measure the impact of the west from a starting point of Africa untouched, no one has ever succeeded in finding a satisfactory definition of baseline Africa. In more recent historical work, the search has been abandoned. One important new line of interpretation originates not in African studies itself but in European and world history, and this approach makes the problem of a baseline much less significant. This is the idea of a developing modern world system, emanating from Europe and exercising early and decisive constraints on autonomous African development.

The modern world system approach, by stressing a much earlier European impact and reducing the autonomous role of African agency, has reduced the threefold scheme into a three-phase development, something like this:

8. slave trade   colonial domination   neocolonialism

In this scheme, there is no available baseline, at least not one that matters. There are no longer three distinct stages, but a continuous process, with three phases. In all three phases, the impact of Europe is a destructive one, as the capitalist power of core countries develops at the expense of the periphery—Africa. If African agencies are really helpless, African history itself becomes less significant, what African historians do less important.

Just on the level of the significance of their work, Africanists are not inclined fully to accept this argument. Again, it is one which stimulates new insight and good new work. But it also stimulates its own reaction. Did not Africans themselves have the energy, market responsiveness, entrepreneurial values, and acquisitiveness to hold their own in trade? Researchers then find these realities in the African past—and present.

9. precolonial period   colonial rule   independence

African enterprise and market responsiveness

This scheme would break into two types—one in which colonial rule was judged to place a destructive squeeze on African enterprise, the other taking colonial rule to be too weak and inefficient to put down African entrepreneurs even though failing to help them much. The scheme reverses the previous formulation that shows European influence to be overwhelmingly destructive and oppressive at all stages.

In these latter schemes, the threefold sequence has really been abandoned, and the continuity of African history is brought out more than ever. European contact is of longer duration, the baseline of Africa untouched more remote and harder to locate. Then too, the third phase, present-day Africa, the thing to be explained, is no longer the Africa of optimistic, newly independent nations. It is the Africa of dislocation, underdevelopment, and famine. In these models, the ongoing process, not the fixed reality of a specious present is brought into focus.

These schemes and this discussion are a help, I hope, to students trying to read African history. African history, they find out, is more than simply all that information. They learn, too, that each approach is not so much right or wrong as incomplete; and that even if two approaches are contradictory—say, the model of colonial exploitation and that of colonial development—that they can still learn something of value from both.

Then, too, students who had felt a need for justifying and defending African history can test these various interpretive strategies against a variety of reading. If this approach to learning African history succeeds, I hope it will make them more critical readers, and I hope it will help them outgrow the apologetic posture, a posture African history no longer needs. To continue the commitment to apologetic strategies would now, it seems to me, only place limits on the increase of understanding of the African past.

But far from fading away, apologetic strategies have seen a recent resurgence. The new style could be called the *apologetics of precedence*. In this line of argument, the apologist claims prior credit for certain human achievements. Egyptian civilization, the first in the world, was a black African civilization. Cleopatra was an African. The Greeks derived, in fact stole, their culture from the original Egyptian achievements. These ideas have been around for a century or so, but they have recently assumed new prominence as one of the central points of 'Afrocentric' doctrine.

On one level the claim is trivial. A glance at the map indicates clearly that Egypt is in Africa. Then, too, the affinity of Egyptian with other African cultures is widely recognized and is scarcely controversial. It is the specifically racial content of the claim that raises problems. When people are busy scrutinizing Egyptian art to determine the skin color of the figures, we begin to sense something is wrong.

Part of what is wrong is that in answering the old racist charge that Africa has no history and never achieved anything, the apologist accepts the categories and assumptions of the racist scholarship. The racists were wrong in their conclusions. But more than that, their entire project was fallacious.

The first fallacious assumption of the racists—perpetuated in the apologetics of precedence—is that the human race is divided into discrete, permanent groups that maintain their separate identity through time, somewhat like colored balls on a snooker table. Thus, the divisions and groups of our century can be traced back all the way to ancient times, where the same divisions existed. I do not believe the ancient Egyptians would know what we were talking about.

A second dubious argument is that human groups need to have creative achievement of certain sorts to their credit in order for their quality and human worth to be validated. Again, the original racist mistake is perpetuated in the arguments posed in reply.

In combination, these two fallacies were a cornerstone of racist ideology. This kind of racist argument was founded on a cultural-biological linkage, with certain races capable of certain kind of achievements.

A third and related fallacy is that creation and invention are positive whereas borrowing from other peoples is negative. This was part of the racist attack on Africa, that Africans were good imitators only, not capable of originality. The apologetic answer has retained this feature but added a twist. Borrowing, as the Greeks from the Egyptians, can be seen as a kind of theft, an appropriating of someone else's heritage. Thus, European scholars are seen as giving the Greeks—whites—credit for something they did not create.

The scholars of Afrocentrism sometimes move from defense to attack in their argument that the general silence of most ancient historians about blacks in the ancient world is itself part of a racist enterprise.

Again, as with other apologetics, some valuable work came out of the project of answering the racist attack on Africa. And, at least at one time, it was certainly necessary to answer this attack. Now, it seems to me, it is time to move on. The best way of doing this is to jettison the whole framework created in that racist scholarship. I am not, I want to emphasize, calling the scholars who claim that Egypt is an African civilization racist. I am saying that the debate over the African identity of ancient Egyptians, viewed narrowly in racial terms, is no longer very interesting or worthwhile. The claims assume an automatic link between race and culture that, again, comes down from earlier scholarship and is discredited today.

William McNeill has suggested one way to proceed when he argues the stimulus that occurs in zones of contact between groups. Certainly, the ancient Nile valley was such a zone. Peoples mingled;

new challenges arose. Borrowing *and* creativity, creative borrowing, 'stimulus diffusion,' by which a people could borrow an idea and invent from it an entirely new artifact—these are the kinds of things McNeill says we should expect in such a zone.

In an investigation of Egyptian history framed along these lines, we would need to examine, in a historical setting, what groups were present and what identities existed at that time. But since the human race is not divided into permanent, discrete groups, any attempt to identify the historical groups with our own, we and they fashion, is bound to be unhistorical. And, further, since no one can doubt the ability and creative genius of all groups, this question of staking out claims to given creations and inventions does not really matter.

I can anticipate some severe criticisms of this argument. The Afrocentric approach, of which the Africanness of ancient Egypt is a part, has been put forward as a means of instilling pride and fostering identity among African-American students. Racism has done enormous damage in the past to the self-esteem of this population. Whatever will be effective in repairing that damage, by all means should be done.

I believe that we can do better than such a polemical and one-dimensional use of history. I have no interpretation of ancient Egyptian history to offer in place of the Afrocentric one. Maybe, couched in different terms, it could have substantial value. But I do not think it should be announced as a doctrine or a litmus test of commitment. The history of ancient Egypt, the processes by which that civilization was formed and developed are rich and complex. Let students immerse themselves in the sources and literature of that history. Let them test, discuss, and explore the material. Let them examine, question, and probe the assumptions of this or other interpretations. Even if agreement on a 'correct' interpretation of Egyptian history—or any other subject—is never achieved, that process, that struggle to understand, may well accomplish many of the goals that the Afrocentric approach aimed at.

My way is harder, slower, less sure. It offers no quick results. It has the advantage that it is for no one group. We are all the heirs of all of history, and that history is endlessly rich and complex. History offers many chances for insight and understanding, not just a few simple symbols. A probing, mind-expanding, Gandhian pursuit of historical knowledge is, it seems to me, a pride-engendering task for anyone.

NOTES

1. Reprinted from the poem "Answer," in the book *Christmas in Biafra and other Poems*, by Chinua Achebe. © 1971, 1973 by Chinua Achebe. Doubleday Anchor Books, 1973. Used by permission of the author.

2. Reprinted from the book, *Return to My Native Land*, by Aime Césaire, Penguin Books, 1969. Used by permission of Presence Africaine.

12

The Other:
The Problem of Authenticity

> . . . discover
> The differences of degree that separate
> One view from the other, and so celebrate
> The fortunate variance, the happy fall,
> And light to contemplate the difference by.
>
> Josephine Miles, *Collected Poems*.[1]

My students want to know about the other culture, and curriculum planners require that they should be exposed to such matters. Though we are sitting in an American classroom, we need somehow to gain direct access to the society we are studying. What is needed is some reading material to purvey the realities of the other society in its own authentic voice.

This is, indeed, an important part of an education in pluralism. One major thrust of the scholarship in the last thirty years in African history has been to view Africa from the inside and not merely as Europeans viewed it. The use of African evidence and the analysis of African experience has been the hallmark of a great deal of writing on African history. This parallels a more general concern that history should include more than the story of political leaders, the powerful, the successful, the articulate. Evidence about the victims of history, ordinary people, the colonized, the inarticulate of the world is vital to any rounded account of the past, and the enterprise and ingenuity of historians in reconstructing these stories from sparse and ambiguous evidence has been a triumph of recent scholarship.

I do not question any of this. My commitment is also to let these voices be heard. But the difficulties of putting this kind of evidence

over to students are formidable. One group of students has a whole
set of detailed and strong expectations and ideas about the qualities
of this voice and the contents of its message. When I present documents and readings for class discussion, I find these preconceived
notions stand in the way of the inquiries I want to pursue. The
students assume, first, the same fixed and easy distinctions between
the colonizer and the colonized, between First World and Third,
between ourselves and the others. Again, as so often, they understand
the matter and I want to understand.

There is perhaps a larger group of students who are more passive,
who do not have answers to the question because they do not realize
there is any question to be asked. They want information, but most
of them tend quickly to be converted to the point of view of the
more activist students.

In chapter 4, I identified myself as an outsider, in contrast to
various possible insider identities. My argument there was that
although an outsider could never fully grasp and describe insider
realities in their full complexity, he or she could still teach and
discuss those subjects. The outsider's perspective was still useful,
though different, from that of insiders. In any case, I concluded,
the right of outsiders to discuss any aspect of human affairs was
undeniable and beyond question.

Here, I shift my angle of vision. 'The voice of the other' that
I am now talking about is a piece of evidence by which to provide
access into that 'inside' reality. My students confidently expect this
can be accomplished. I say only that it can be tried. My hope, in
fact, is to subvert these simple categories of colonizer and colonized,
outsider and insider, ourselves and the other, and of discrete cultural
entities that have defined and fixed boundaries. Perhaps I can
accomplish this by presenting for discussion a series of documents
that are *possibly* authentic articulations of the other, and to explore
what this phrase could possibly mean anyway. Perhaps this will at
least call into question the students' facile expectations and make
their world more complicated, destroying those easy categories of
authenticity and otherness—at least in their most naive forms.

Steven Feierman, in his book *Peasant Intellectuals*, summarizes
succinctly the dilemmas inherent in the entire anthropological
enterprise:

> The problem of otherness is not easily solved, for the
> subject matter of anthropology is cultural difference. If

we define the people of a given society as different from us, then we have defined them as other, distant from us, not subject to the same historical forces or living in the same moral universe. This is unacceptable. But if we say that we are indeed coeval, living in the same era, subject to the same historical forces, struggling with the same issues, then we lose the picture of cultural variation which is the heart of anthropology. (p. 38)

It is, then, a back and forth game we have to play in considering others' accounts of themselves. They are like us or not like us; we do not know in advance and we have to inquire. Furthermore, we can find in the other society not one voice but a great variety. Preconceived tests of authenticity will only lead us astray.

Last year I had my South African history class read Tim Keegan's book, *Facing the Storm*. Based on evidence gathered in the Witwatersrand Oral Documentation Project, it portrays the lives of four ordinary black South African farmers. The book provides full family backgrounds reaching back into the nineteenth century, and it continues the account into the 1980s. Here are stories of struggles for survival in the face of ever increasing and relentless oppression and hardship. Keegan takes us well beyond the usual accounts of laws, high politics, even mass demonstrations and political movements, to render a vivid picture of ordinary lives in extraordinary conditions.

Many of the students did not like the book. We had long arguments, and I gradually came to understand what bothered them. Their notions were, I remain convinced, wrongheaded and mistaken, but their stubbornness in them pointed me toward a major pedagogical campaign.

Students, first of all, felt cheated. The voice of the book was that of Tim Keegan, not of his African informants. The methodological sophistication of the book did not cut any ice at all. What was Keegan up to? Was he telling us all about these African lives or holding something back? "Historians commonly write their books from primary sources; why does this common procedure bother you in this case?," I inquired. "Would the African farmers speak to him openly?," they asked me. This was as close as I could get; no one would go any farther—Tim Keegan was *white*, and his book could not provide the authentic voice they were expecting. That, at any rate, is my interpretation of student concerns, though I know they would never be willing to confirm this suspicion.

Besides, I only wanted to argue that Tim Keegan's was a valuable and successful book. I will admit that it does not render the 'authentic voice of the other'. But then, what does? What would such a document be? A colleague of mine, teaching a general course, had included Jamaica Kincaid's *A Small Place*. "To represent 'the other' "he said. "How do you know?" I asked him.

I suspect that I will never find the answer to the question. To keep trying is to tap into the rich variety of human experience, and that is more fruitful than arriving at easy conclusions. The presentation of a wide variety of documents for class discussion, therefore, will remain one of my standard classroom techniques. But to say, "This is the authentic voice of the other," is to know the significance and status of the document in question, and significance and status are just what I want to discuss. These are the very things that can never be settled in advance.

Dinesh D'Souza raises a similar issue in *Illiberal Education*. He notes that a highly popular reading for the multicultural curriculum across the country is the book *I, Rigoberta Menchu*. Here, surely, is the authentic voice of a Guatemalan peasant woman. Not so, D'Souza points out. Here is a very unusual Guatemalan peasant woman, one who has traveled to France and tells her story in the language of Marxism. Her vocabulary and consciousness are, surely, not typical in Guatemalan villages.

Dinesh D'Souza has a point. My experience has been that the students expect a certain content and tone. If their expectations are confirmed, then they know they are hearing the 'authentic voice of the other'. To meet their tests of authenticity, the document in question must be militant, revolutionary, Fanonian, and politically hostile to the West. The preference is also for a full commitment to indigenous culture and hostility to Western culture. Not every document reflects these attitudes, and can, to the extent it falls short, be judged inauthentic. Some documents are judged to reflect the attitudes of a 'self-hating' individual, or false consciousness, or the contamination of western cultural influence.

Student discussions of the documents I pass out in class put me in mind of the photographer Edward Curtis, who scratched the images of western artifacts off of the negatives of his Native American photographs.

And that is cheating. Such self-confirming prejudgments stand in the way of understanding the world as it is. There is in fact no one 'other', but a vastly complex and everchanging cultural mix, in which Western influence is nearly always a factor. Africa untouched, as we have seen, cannot be found in the past, and it certainly cannot be found in the complex and turbulent present. (And I must note that even this statement is inadequate, for 'the West' is another conceptual shortcut, and the cultures of European peoples have been formed from diverse influences over millennia.)

That is why, to return to the Guatemalan example, Dinesh D'Souza is wrong, as wrong as the people he is criticizing. Rigoberta Menchu is not a typical Guatemalan peasant, but she is a possible one and an interesting one. D'Souza shares with his opponents the futile quest for the typical voice that can be judged authentic. Perhaps a more 'typical' outcome would have been Menchu's death and the silencing of her voice.

In my class, to get past this problem of what is typical, I will need to present a great variety of documents for discussion. None of them can be judged the 'authentic other' by any uniform test. But they all do, for otherness is not one single set of characteristics. People are alike and different in ever varying and unexpected ways. Each document presents new problems of interpretation. They all need evaluation and discussion to yield their meaning.

Novels, autobiographies and memoirs, political manifestoes, proverbs, traditional and modern poetry, editorials, African hymns and religious writings—all are suitable for circulation and discussion. I am interested not in defining a fixed 'African perspective' but in noting the variety of perspectives, through the period from precolonial, to colonial, and independent Africa. I am interested in the distinctions from region to region and from one African people to another. If we have the chance to go into more detail, the variety of statements from a single time and place are worth noting—Africa is complicated, like other human societies.

With any given document before us, there is a lot to talk about. Under whose auspices and by what chain of circumstances do we acquire this document? What selectors (including myself, the teacher), editors, translators, interpreters, interested parties have brought it to us? We cannot always answer all of these questions or measure the difference the answers might make. But at least we can note that such things might matter.

Again, we need to consider the author. For what purpose was the text created? For what audience? These questions are often somewhat easier and can yield interesting answers—or guesses. But, again, firm and detailed answers matter less than noting the concerns.

When we move to the social situation depicted in the document, students are more comfortable. But, I tell them, the society depicted in the document is (for a contemporaneous document) a society in which this document exists. The message of the document comes not only from what it says but in its very existence. For example, the racist situation described in one document has to include and take account of the description and critique of racism contained in the document. What difference, in other words, does it make that the given racist society itself produces this description and critique? I dwell on these aspects of interpretation, because students most easily and commonly use the documents I present as transparent windows through which to view the society they are studying. They tend to read African novels, for example, purely as sources of information, forgetting considerations of author and audience or of the difficulties of defining the status of the document itself. They are stubborn about this. I try even to bribe them into considering something else. "The student who considers the possible message or purpose of the author in relation to an audience will come across as a genius," I say. But when I read the papers no one will have done so.

A few years ago I used Sol Plaatje's novel, *Mhudi*, and all of these problems came up. Plaatje, one of the founders of the ANC, wrote the novel about 1920, and the novel recounts events of the 1830s. Halley's comet figured in the action of the novel,and its next appearance was a few years before *Mhudi* was written. Plaatje had written an article about the comet's impact on Africans at that time. And the comet was visible yet again as we were reading the book in the 1980s. The presence of the comet symbolized nicely, I thought, the three chronological and three critical points of view by which the novel could be evaluated. But despite numerous suggestions, cajoling, and bribes, the students only wrote about the 1830s, with the novel as their source of information.

Plaatje's novel is about the possibility that might have existed in the 1830s that black and white could live in South Africa as equal partners—and it presents, too, a dark and apocalyptic speech by Mzilikazi, the Ndebele king, warning against common cause with the Europeans as a road to slavery. And it was written at a time when those who had been raised on the hopes, as Plaatje had, faced a bleak future indeed, when Mzilikazi's warnings seemed about to be confirmed. And we were reading at a time when the struggle between the ANC Plaatje had helped found and the Apartheid state was entering its final crisis, giving the book a rich new context.

Yet one group of students saw nothing but some information about the Great Trek, while another suspected Plaatje of being a traitor to the cause of Third World solidarity.

The task, then, is to get students to look for meaning on more than one level as they read. Such closer reading is required to grasp and appreciate some of the richness of a book like *Mhudi*. And this complicated, nuanced, detailed interpretation of documents may lead some students to rethink preconceived definitions of authenticity and to admit complexity, ambiguity, and irony into their thinking about subjects like African history.

To me, African history is a branch of human history in all its glory, tragedy, ambiguity, and complexity. It is a difficult topic and worth a lifetime of study. To reduce it to 'heritage', and to a source of 'values' or a set of moral symbols and lessons is to sell the subject seriously short. This is what I fear some proponents of Afrocentrism tend to do in their approach to the subject. In my discussions with them, Afrocentricity sometimes seems to be a set of tests of authenticity, defined in advance. The ironic result is that some African authors and historical actors do not pass the test.

I do not, however, wish simply to attack and condemn Afrocentrism, but rather have ongoing interesting debates with its advocates. I will argue that in the complex interplay between Africa and Europe, which is so powerfully formative in African history, there is no easy lining up of heroes and villains. Setting up a contest and scoring points for their side and our side is not a productive way to teach and study. Lining up indigenous inventions for which to claim credit while at the same time repudiating outside influences is apologetic and, at bottom, unnecessary.

African history, in all its richness, is its own justification. Making it into didactic lessons and moral symbols is to patronize our students. The documents I pass out in class will, I hope, make students consider complexity and ambiguity, while avoiding quick conclusions. Rather than label an African author or historical figure as hero or villain too quickly, we need to consider the situation he or she was in. Rather than worry about whether the documents we are examining provide an authentic voice, we need to get students to carry on a kind of Gandhian conversation with them, in which no final answer as to the meaning or status of the document can ever be achieved, but in which the student can gain new levels of understanding through close reading and rereading.

This is hard intellectual labor. Occasionally, for some students—or teachers—the reward can be a moment of epiphany, as they, we, suddenly gain a vivid sense of others' lives and mentalities, even across deep divides of culture and experience. This kind of sudden insight can be moving, exciting, upsetting, enlightening, funny, even possibly unpleasant. Living in our world raises these emotions; it seems appropriate that education about that world should do so, too.

NOTE

1. Reprinted from the poem beginning, "So you are thinking of principles," in Josephine Miles, *Kinds of Affection*, copyright 1967 by Josephine Miles, Wesleyan University Press reprinted by permission of the University Press of New England.

13

The World Context of American Pluralism

> ... both sides
> Have to step back from private dreams of power
> And listen to the soft voice of reason
> Singing its one-line song,
> Which should be easy to memorize
> Though it hasn't caught on yet
> And won't be popular.
>
> Carl Dennis, "That Poem," *The Outskirts of Troy.*[1]

Some of the courses I teach at Stony Brook fulfill a requirement called "the world beyond European traditions." This bureaucratic phrase addresses the need of American students to know about cultures and ways of life markedly different from their own—or so I understand the intentions of the educators who framed the requirement.

To study these ways of life is well and good, but history keeps getting in the way. In South Asia and Southeast Asia, the Pacific, the Levant, Eastern Europe, and parts of Africa, conflicts between communities in plural societies have reached an extreme form. Lord Durham's 1839 description of Canada, "two nations warring in the bosom of a single state," could be multiplied many times over for some of the countries in these regions.

A major component of the twentieth-century history of these regions is turbulence, riots, massacres, and war. The study of these conflicts makes many of my students uncomfortable. They are keyed to the colonizer-colonized model, and bloody carnage between groups of colonized people is hard to accept. Is my raising of these

issues a sneaky endorsement of the imperialists? A good question—
imperialists tried to justify themselves in just this way. Again, is one
of the conflicting parties doing the bidding of the colonizer? What
about the ways of life students expected to learn about?

Here is pluralism with a vengeance, pluralism in the sense of
conflict between religious, linguistic, or racial communities in Third
World societies. I suspect this is not the material that educational
planners had in mind, but its study, it seems to me, is of overwhelming importance as part of an education in pluralism.

Students also have to take courses in the category, American
Pluralism, and my courses do not meet that requirement. But if any
such set of requirements at American colleges and universities is
to make sense, connections have to be made between the United
States and the rest of the world. The problems of diversity in the
United States can only be understood in a world perspective. The
United States' impact on the world is one source of conflicts in the
world, and we import the diversity and some of the conflicts.
Domestic and foreign spheres are inseparable.

Having said that, the extent of United States diversity—and of
conflicts between cultural, racial, religious, and linguistic communities—is slight and muted by the standards of other world
regions. Aside from anything else, these conflicts around the world
provide a series of lessons, mostly negative, as we pursue the task
of shaping a pluralist United States. I will refer briefly below to the
causes of conflict. My main topic is the various 'solutions' that have
been tried, historically, to control conflict in plural societies.

I begin with a bald list of unpleasant alternatives:

a. genocide
b. expulsion (the standard euphemism is 'population transfer')
c. forced assimilation
d. federalism
e. other constitutional mechanisms (communal electorates,
   fancy franchises, reserved offices)
f. partition
g. secularism (I refer to Nehru's claim that the state would not
   exert power on behalf of the interests of any community and
   that therefore political support need not be mounted on the
   basis of communal interests. Nehru's claim is merely a way
   of wishing the conflict away.)

h. imperial rule (the provision of impartial arbitration by the imperial power, which offers evenhanded justice for all communities)

Historically, for many centuries, imperial rule was far and away the most important mechanism for controlling conflict between communities in diverse societies—even as the conquest of large scale states with urban centers of trade and administration created the extended societies that brought diverse communities together. The imperial claim was that only the ruler could be just to all communities. In the premodern, preindustrial centuries, this claim was more or less effective, though I would not idealize those past societies, and the mechanism of 'impartial imperial arbitration' is not recoverable in today's world.

This claim of impartiality was asserted also by the European colonial empires of the nineteenth and twentieth centuries. But in the end, it was a claim these empires could not genuinely sustain. First, they were racist empires. As the metropolitan societies became increasingly democratic, racism served as the 'premise of inequality' by which imperial rule could be justified and the implications of democracy denied in the dependent societies. But the liberal ideologies of the metropolis leaked out into the colonial societies anyway, and this was an important source of inspiration (though not the only one) for resistance to colonial rule. If settlers came to a colonial territory in any numbers claiming the special privileges of racial dominance, the contradictions between metropolitan liberalism and imperial ideology were greatly increased.

Nevertheless, in the late nineteenth and early twentieth centuries, European colonial powers were damping down intercommunity conflict and smugly asserting that this service justified their rule. To see more clearly why their claim was not valid, it is necessary to look briefly at the causes of 'communal' conflict. The argument of the time was between two interpretations: that it was caused by ancient, primordial enmities, tribalism, ancestral hatreds, and the like; or, alternatively, that it was fomented by devious imperialist 'divide and rule' tactics. (My students always enthusiastically latch onto this latter idea.)

I try to develop a much more complex analysis of the causes of conflict, posed between these extremes. These were empires like no previous ones, capitalist empires ruled by industrializing powers.

The social change imperial rule and the imperial economy engendered was explosive, and the 'leakage' of metropolitan ideas has to be seen in this context. I can again only provide a brief list of some of the forces operating in the colonies under European rule. While something like 'divide and rule' mechanisms might sometimes have been present, far and away more important was sheer inadvertence. I would look at these matters, for example:

a. The differential impact of western education and other new techniques and sources of power and opportunity on the various communities of the colonized population.
b. Labor mobility in a capitalist economy, creating new contacts between groups—and this a worldwide process, not confined to one colonial territory. Not only the overseas Europeans and the overseas Africans, but also the overseas Chinese and the overseas Indians are the products of this process. The presence of these migrant groups led to explosive social tensions in numerous territories of Africa, the Caribbean, the Pacific, and Southeast Asia.
c. In colonial territories, the implications of representative politics, as new institutions are gradually introduced in the late colonial period. Instead of forgetting about traditional identities, as Nehru expected, many leaders politicized their particular tradition and recruited followers on its basis. This was a means, especially, for substantially westernized leaders to validate their leadership in the eyes of the general population with whom they had otherwise little in common.

European colonial empires were caught in such rapid social and economic change that they could not maintain any claim of stable, impartial rule. These empires were destroyed by their own contradictions.

This is a bald summary the kind of analysis I pursue in some of the courses I teach. When we look at these situations in detail, students are surprised at how hard it is to assess blame or to assign the easy labels of villain and victim. These are tough, knotty, social problems, and sometimes the outcomes are tragic.

At this stage of American history, it behooves us to increase our awareness of these problems, of these histories. Our own divisions, our own problems of pluralism, are relatively slight and muted by these standards, though I recognize that some of those deeply involved in these issues will disagree.

The experiment in American higher education to devise a curriculum based on pluralism is, in effect, part of still another strategy for overcoming conflict in a diverse society. The project of confronting *pluralism* in education seems to be based on the hope that students can be taught to accept, value, preserve, and even celebrate various kinds of diversity within a common society. It is a kind of social engineering through education, and I am dubious about the effectiveness of such efforts.

I do not mean these efforts are futile. I have devoted my entire career in teaching to this kind of endeavor and to these issues, and I believe that education has an important role in helping our society come to terms with its increasing diversity. But expectations are pitched much too high, and too many people expect rapid and dramatic results. I expect results to be incremental, gradual, and partial. Education by itself can, perhaps, deepen some people's sympathy, knowledge, and understanding.

My fear, in short, is that the means are feeble in relation to the problem—even though, as I have said, the United States version of diversity-based conflicts is muted by world standards. We need to remember that often—and this is one of the lessons I try to put across in some of my courses—the ethnic, racial, linguistic or religious identities may provide the badges and symbols of conflict but are not necessarily what the conflict is *about*. When we study these conflicts, one of the important questions, always, is to what extent the ethnic divisions are correlated with differing access to quality education, to economic opportunity, and to positions of power in the society under study.

In the case of the United States, this implies that consciousness, toleration, and even celebration of diversity may not be sufficient. And that dealing with these issues only in the educational arena may not be sufficient. The reason that the 'American Pluralism' approach seems plausible—and perhaps even the reason conflict in the United States seems 'muted'—is that power in the society is distributed very unevenly indeed. Some of my colleagues have suggested that it would not be enough to achieve in the curriculum a kind of salutary 'fairness' to all groups. 'Multicultural' curricula, which in some schools mean little more than rearranging and relabelling existing courses, often serves only this very limited purpose. Schools adopting such curricula want to 'look good', but they need also to face tough educational problems. A more difficult and urgent goal, for example, would be to help people, especially from the hitherto dominant groups, to break out of their own parochialism and out of the complacency of being on top.

It is well to remember, too, that our educational efforts will operate in a situation in which claims of impartial imperial arbitration, schemes of forced assimilation, and accusations that ethnic identity is itself the cause of conflict and is somehow therefore 'unamerican', are still being made. To be more than tokenism, what we do has to take these realities into account.

To study inter-community conflict in Indian, Indonesian, Fijian, Malayan, Sri Lankan or other histories is, among other things, to arm ourselves with a knowledge of past mistakes, past tragedies, past injustices, that we may not repeat them in our own society. The importance of South African history for this same purpose I address in another essay.

The society of the United States is not automatically immune from the kinds of breakdown that have occurred elsewhere. The experiment of an education in pluralism is an attempt to avoid the extremes of forced assimilation and rampant separatism that some fear. Whether it will succeed I do not know. As a teacher, it is all I have to offer.

NOTE

1. From *The Outskirts of Troy*, © 1988 by Carl Dennis. Used by permission of William Morrow & Company Inc.

14

Learning in the Pluralist Classroom

Each morning
The past is that much longer,
All our mistakes recorded
On yet another page.
This is the book the burdened heart cannot unlearn.

And the future
With its somber promises
And bright betrayals
Inscrutably beckoning.
We move toward it, the way no briefer than before.

Daniel Hoffman, "The Way," *The Center of Attention.*[1]

One of the slogans of conservative, back-to-basics school reformers is "chronological history." The slogan implies that history should be taught in a straightforward, objective, factual, no-nonsense manner. Students should simply learn the information. The accusation of these conservatives is that the social studies curriculum has been watered down and burdened with so many 'points of view' and 'perspectives' that students simply do not know very much.

I am on neither side in this debate. On the one hand, these essays have dwelt on disagreements, arguments, and contrasting perspectives. On the other hand, the task of teaching and learning historical information is an important part of what I am doing, and I must make this explicit.

I do not endorse the approach of those calling for "chronological history." Though we perforce must live our lives in chronological time, we do not really understand our lives chronologically and that may not always be the most effective way to study history. And I hope to arrive at some better ways to learn and remember information than the old 'text-recitation' approach. My guess is that the demands I want to make on students are greater, not less, than in that approach. For me, learning information is only a starting point. Going beyond that to thinking about and making use of the information is what really counts. And this process is also a way to learn facts by making them significant. If information, a sequence of dates for example, is presented as a crucial part of an argument it then becomes memorable so that it need not be memorized in the old sense.

To define my own approach more clearly in contrast to the traditional one that conservative critics want to reestablish, I will outline two contrasting models of teaching: the traditional classroom, with the teacher in authority imparting a body of information; and a more open classroom, with the teacher as a leader of discussion. I will call this classroom *pluralist*. So far as I know, the word has not been used in this sense and will perhaps not be burdened with associations as the "open," "inquiry," or "discovery" labels would be. What I am looking for does not quite fit these terms as they have been used. The "pluralist" approach also depends on a body of information. The exercises in reading and interpretation I will describe are not undertaken instead of the information but in addition to it. Pluralist seems a suitable name because the variety of perspectives and experiences of the students is a benefit, not an obstacle, to the goals being pursued in teaching.

A crude outline of the "traditional" classroom could be given as follows: First, this approach is based on a *tabula rasa* theory of knowledge. To know is to acquire information, which can be imparted by someone who has it. Authority is then the primary source of knowledge. How to gain knowledge through reason and observation may be taught, but these skills too are imparted by authority. The teacher tells the student, then the student knows.

What are the implications of this model of teaching? First, the teacher as *authority* must have authority in the sense of control. Subject organization is locked by the fact that the teacher must be prepared with the right information. Hence curriculum plans and subject organization are sacrosanct. And given the assumption about how knowledge is acquired, the values imparted by the teacher must be sound, orthodox, and correct. Evaluation by examination can take the form of recitation-testing: does the student know what she has been told? Reading is a passive process of receiving the printed word and learning what the authority says. Even esthetic creativity can be reduced to rules for students to learn. As a result of this education, we know "answers." Our thinking is set in tracks, so that curricular subject divisions tend to govern the things that we associate together. This description is crude and exaggerated but does, I believe, describe in outline some of the assumptions of the educational system many people went through in midtwentieth century America. We read passively; we test for information; we think in tracks without making fresh associations. Our mind may be divided into logic-tight compartments in that we hold opinions incompatible with information that we have learned.

In the pluralist classroom, on the other hand, the basic assumptions of the traditional system are reversed. The theory of knowledge is platonic—not that we literally believe in innate ideas, but merely that each individual has a mindset, an intellectual context, a circle of experience, so that he or she can learn by drawing on and shaping this as well as by receiving new data. The process of education then becomes a continuous confronting of this mindset with new evidence, data, information, and ways of looking at things. The new data modifies our outlook but is also given meaning by it. The teacher, as in any classroom, will impart information, but the students do not just learn that information. Each interprets the information. The teacher speaks from a certain circle of experience, which differs from those of the students, just as the students' differ from each other. The class can communicate because the circles of experience overlap, but each message means something a little different to each person who hears it, because the context, while overlapping, is a little different for each person.

All these things are, to be sure, happening in any classroom, even the most traditional one. But instead of ignoring, bypassing, or trying to overcome the diverse responses, I want to acknowledge them and make use of them.

A group with entirely homogeneous intellectual contexts would find communication easy but would almost not need to undertake it. Such a class, with all members sharing a single perspective, might spend their time celebrating and confirming their agreement. A group with overlapping but diverse contexts would find communication difficult (because of the diversity) but interesting and rewarding (also because of the diversity). In this class, there might be friction, but the potential for learning is great. If there is no overlapping of context, if the teacher cannot attach her material to something the students know about, or if the students are too heterogeneous, then communication becomes overwhelmingly difficult.

When the teacher says something, the impact of what she says is not the same as she expects. A student might be able to tell her something about what she said that she did not know herself. The teacher must therefore listen as well as talk. Even if a teacher thought he knew the truth, he would have to realize that he could not impart it simply by stating it, because his conviction that he holds the truth is supported by a complex set of associations. Each statement he makes is removed from his context and will float loose until it is placed in a new context by each listener. The teacher cannot avoid this by imparting his whole circle of experience—not at least without at first breaking down the mindsets of the students, an attempt that would lead either to docility or rebellion. This is why the teacher cannot be the authoritative source of truth.

If the teacher is learning something herself and cannot (therefore, need not) impart a uniform and homogeneous blanket of truth onto the students, then she can afford to give up her authority position without being defensive. This is a risky and difficult venture for the teacher. The teacher must be willing to say, "I do not know, but I want to understand," thereby shedding the security blanket of omniscience. What the teacher can then do is lead a class in the process of finding things out by asking important questions. How many times have we teachers reacted deep down to a sharp (i.e., intelligent) question, by saying to ourselves that it is really an impertinent interruption, using up time we need for imparting information? That is defensiveness; the reason for our discomfiture is that we believe that to have any ignorance revealed is to threaten our position of authority.

Someone already might object that facts are facts, and there can be no argument about them. At least they can be given authoritatively. This is true, but in this approach the dispensing of information becomes only the easiest and most trivial part of the teachers' task. A greater time and effort will go into making unexpected connections, testing a variety of interpretations, engaging the students' ideas and values while still remaining strongly focused on the given subject. We want, in short, to argue history not simply narrate it.

What the conservative, 'chronological history' reformers often do not admit is that even the soberest factual narrative is an interpretive, selection-arrangement of historical information and inevitably uses conceptual and evaluative language with no real basis in archival sources. I want my students to be able to see these aspects of any historical account they might read, to spot the conjectures and to be suspicious, even as they learn facts.

Other implications can be drawn from the original premise of a 'platonic' theory of knowledge. The teacher does not need authority; facts lose their primacy in the sense that simple recitation of a body of information is not enough. The result of education, rather than a knowledge of 'answers,' locked thinking, and an attempt to duplicate the last generation in the next, becomes instead a knowledge of questions, intellectual autonomy, the next generation allowed to be itself. And students of varying backgrounds and perspectives will not be forced to conform to a single version of history but will remain free to draw varying conclusions and lessons from the historical conversation they have held in common.

Implications of this 'platonic' theory are especially important for reading. The process of reading is complex and central in this whole endeavor. One can still read for information, with the book as an authority. But one can also read actively for reaction, not just passively to receive data. That is, the significance of what you read is governed at least partly by what you know already, your existing context, not just by what the author thinks is significant. Thus, whether an author's values are orthodox or not is less important than in the authority-centered system of education. We are teaching critical reading, not passive acceptance of assignments.

This concept of reading seems to be rare nowadays. Few are willing to have students read material they might disagree with. All seem to want textbooks to follow one or another orthodoxy. Will students sheltered in these ways be prepared to deal with life in a conflicted world?

On the college level, certainly, students should be made to read more critically and suspiciously. A communist or even a racist author, a revolutionary, a conservative, a liberal, can each be tested against the intellectual context of the student.

Some will certainly fear that some students will uncritically accept pernicious and evil doctrines from such reading. It is possible that some students will be affected in unexpected ways, but not in any consistent direction. They are as likely to react against material as to swallow it whole. The revolutionary reading might make one student more conservative, one more radical, and lack much impact on another. And some may regard the exposing of students to racist writings as a shocking idea. Such writing must, of course, be placed in context and sensitively discussed. I have seen students helped to overcome their own hidden racist feelings in the course of such assignments.

Education is risky. Once we abandon the unrealistic goal of a single result for all, these risks are inevitable, and the advance of critical reading skills is worth it. We are confronting students with a variety of data, trying to develop not a single result for all students but a probing, testing, flexible attitude, in which new information can be assessed constantly, as a mental habit. Tolerance, mental flexibility, lack of defensiveness are traits that I value highly, though there are those who would fear that a loss of fixed conviction might be the result for some students. I answer that fixed conviction still must be tested and confirmed to maintain its value. And while I argue that any given course will not have a consistent or uniform ideological impact on all students, I would probably have to admit that I am peddling liberalism in this entire presentation.

There are also implications in this pluralist classroom approach for the organization of knowledge. The standard divisions of academic subjects are based on a set of arbitrary conventions. History, geography, and economics are concepts, tracks which guide and channel our thinking, categories by which we organize information. Academic departments are institutional limits on the boundaries of inquiry. These boundaries would be a blessing to a teacher-as-imparter-of-information, because they define his responsibility; they may be a bother to a teacher-as-leader-of-inquiry. But I cannot feel too upset about this. A history or social science department affords plenty of room for an 'inquiry' teacher to operate in.

Proponents of the so-called open classroom at one time objected to fixed texts, assignments, and even courses as coercive. Some of my ideas are drawn from theirs, but on the college level I am not worried too much about crushing the free spirits of my students; knowing a body of information is valuable in itself and is certainly necessary if the class is to have a coherent discussion. Even if a teacher is forced by a department or school board to use a traditional, fact-oriented textbook, there are still many possibilities for learning, beyond mastering the facts. Here I come back to the key importance of reading. Students think they already know how to read, but skills in analytical and critical reading can always be further developed. This is perhaps a personal idiosyncrasy in this age of electronic media, but it is my prejudice. Beyond my suggestions, discussed above, for getting students to respond to controversial materials, exercises to develop skills of inquiry and analysis can even be made with an ordinary textbook. If the theory as described holds, each student will get something different from the common reading, and free discussion can still proceed. Some ideas for reading exercises are as follows:

1. Examine some original documents on which a secondary authority rests, to see what the author has done with them.
2. Ask a set of questions in advance, things students want to know, then see whether a textbook account answers them. One can spot omissions, distortions, special purposes or biases of an author. This exercise reduces the tendency to accept the book as an authority. The book may be right as to facts but need not guide our structure of thinking.
3. Use a secondary authority as a primary source. For example, a book written in the 1950s about the Civil War can be used to learn something about the 1950s. Who was the author, and why does he write this book? For what audience, with what 1950s concerns? What are the biases, messages, ideological commitments?
4. Read a book about one subject while thinking about another. I have asked students what they learned about the United States while reading a book about Australia. Students doing this exercise were engaged in a small experiment in comparative history, in which they moved from the unfamiliar to the familiar, to see what new light would be thrown on a topic they already knew something about.

A basic assumption of this approach is that it is terribly difficult to gain and keep individual intellectual autonomy, very easy to accept authority. Cynicism and intolerance are not the same as autonomy but are only outgrowths of defensiveness. Autonomy is never easily gained, never completely achieved, always easily lost—for you, for me, for teachers, for students. But the value of autonomy is great—

the freedom to work on understanding the world in your own way. Education should then be exercises in developing intellectual autonomy by trying to understand the world.

One way to do this is to offer alternatives to the thinking that runs in standard categories by substituting new categories that I or the students can think of. The purpose here is not necessarily to abandon common and familiar ways of looking at things, but rather to develop a greater appreciation for their significance. And when I attempt these experiments, I need to be alert for failures, for connections that are pointless or silly, for presentations that simply do not work. A measure for me of success is whether I am saying things I have said before or saying new things. And the second vital test is whether any such new things are worth saying.

Here I need to provide some examples. I try to take episodes out of their chronological-geographical boxes and put them in thematic boxes. The themes are in effect comparative categories, which enable me to associate together episodes from various chronological-geographical units. I line up the various episodes by themes, in order to examine whether some new insight into their nature and working can be revealed.

The general subject I teach—the contact of expanding Europe with the rest of the world in modern times—lends itself readily to this approach. The themes are comparative, and the practice of comparison, discussed in another essay, serves to release me from the obligation to cover all of modern world history in any one course. I can then look at such themes as plural societies and race relations, imperialism and colonial rule, slavery and other labor systems, intellectual responses to western contact, resistance and collaboration. One episode can stand for others, and students can learn about the processes involved. Ideally, students should find their own themes, but they need to have the idea of having ideas first.

A discussion in my class of the range cattle industry of the trans-Mississippi West demonstrated some of the possibilities of the approach. This subject is familiarly found in the box for American frontier history, pioneer westward movement. I tried placing it in a setting of expansion of Europe, as an example of the process of organizing new regions to produce staple products for the growing metropolitan economy, making it a case analogous to tin in Malaya or tea in Ceylon. The new context for the cowboys did not seem to me that startling, but students were shocked and argumentative, because of the unfamiliarity of the new associations that are evoked. "But the cattlemen were Americans, not European," one student insisted. Recent scholars have pointed out many of them were black. I rest my case.

I am looking for something analogous to the new ways of teaching arithmetic introduced in the 1960s. I learned arithmetic by rote, with base ten taken for granted. After my time, eighth graders came to do problems in base seven, base twelve, or any base. It is not that they would ever use these counting systems, but that the exercise made them conscious of the nature of problem-solving.

In teaching history, we need comparable exercises to jar us out of the familiar mental tracks that keep us from a fuller understanding of history. Many of the 'facts' we learn in traditional historical accounts are not facts at all. Many historical generalizations are couched in conceptual language. I have discussed in another essay some of the difficulties of the terms *nationalism* and *racism*, and that analysis could be extended to many other terms. I often remind students that "concepts are not facts" but are freighted with connotations, values, and emotional implications.

The following are possible exercises to make students and teachers more aware of the conceptual and interpretive nature of historical writing:

1. Periodization—Historical periods are not real but conceptual. Take different themes apart from general history and past politics. Try to divide their development into periods. Use such themes as popular culture, education, aspects of social history. You need something students already know something about.

2. Imagine one thing removed from our lives, say automobiles. What other differences would this make? Start to trace out the technological and institutional interdependences. We could always tell students what influences the automobile has had on modern life. But why do so, when they already know it but do not realize that they do? Find other institutions or artifacts, past or present. Here, too, you need something that students know. This might be used as a method of independent assessment, when students are reading only a standard textbook.

3. I have given students one of the comparative themes mentioned earlier in this essay, say, imperial annexation of overseas territory by European powers. With this category before us, we make a list of questions: What are all of the things we need to know about a case of imperial annexation in order to explain satisfactorily how it came about? Are these questions ones that are answered in the historians' accounts? I gave each student one case of imperial annexation, and we developed an outline of questions together. They found out, I hope, that it would be easy to rig the results in advance by the sort of questions posed. I was trying to convince them that they would be naively trusting if they left the questions to me. Then the class answered the questions for each other, each drawing evidence from one case of imperial annexation. What they learned from each other gradually weaved itself into something close to a history of modern imperialism in its expansive stage. It was fun, and it was hard. It took a semester for only some students to understand what was happening, though all were good at reciting data.

4. I am interested in explanations of timing and location. *When* something happened is a fact. *Why then?* is a question requiring further inquiry. *Where* something happens is a fact. *Why there?* again requires further inquiry. Set down all the things you can think of that might influence or determine the timing of a major event. Why not sooner? Why not later? Why at all? Do the same with location. Do books we read take timing and location for granted, skipping considerations of these questions?

A discussion of the nature of past events could be set in a similar fashion. *What* is it that has happened? Here, we need first to remember that as soon as we define a historical event by attaching a conceptual term to it, we have gone beyond the facts and interpretation has begun. But there is more beyond this. *Why that?* is a next but seldom taken step. For example, William McNeill takes this step when he asks why the territorial state has gained such complete primacy as the major form of ultimate political organization. Most books take this primacy for granted. If we asked students a question to elicit this point, they would be unlikely to answer "territorial state" unless we had taught them this fact by authority.

Yet surely they know it in a more 'platonic' sense but do not realize it or cannot articulate what they know. Greater consciousness of what and how we think, developed by asking questions, leads us to realize things that we had not known we knew.

I need other examples of this kind of exercise, designed to jar our habitual mental associations with new questions and new categories. I cannot think of them freely because, of course, my mind is running along in worn grooves too. Getting and keeping out of these familiar grooves is just as difficult and important for teachers as for students—moreso perhaps.

An obvious difficulty of this entire discussion is that the approach places learning facts in a secondary position, but students cannot participate effectively unless they acquire a lot of historical information. I do not believe that this apparent contradiction is fatal to the approach, but I do believe that it presents a difficulty of application requiring careful thought. Facts, I would say, lose their primacy in defining the subject, but they gain in meaning. Any fact about the past, after all, does not have value or significance in itself. The facts do not speak for themselves. But once facts are selected and arranged then they become significant as evidence for someone's argument about the past. I am placing the primacy on examining the arrangements, models, concepts, principles of selection and organization by which facts about the past are ordered, and we need knowledge of and access to facts to evaluate these strategies. There is no one right way to tell (arrange) the facts of, say, United States history. Students need to be aware of the implications of differing arrangements and selections of information. One arrangement may reveal certain relationships or patterns nicely, but only at the cost of distorting or omitting other things. Reading exercise number one (in which students read some original documents on which a secondary account is based), for example, was designed to show that an author's arrangement is governed by what he wants to say about a topic and does not inhere in the material itself. Students normally think of a strong interpretive line as 'bias,' and a bland factual summary as objective. I disagree: all selection-arrangements are ideologically freighted; some are merely less explicit or less interesting than others.

Access of students to a full body of information such as is available in a textbook is, then, important. Reference exercises are another possibility in filling out students storehouse of factual information. Once students are confronted with a set of questions to answer or an approach they wish to criticize, they can go to atlases, biographical dictionaries, handbooks, encyclopedias, collections of documents—in order to fill out the information they need for their own informed judgments. This could follow after an exercise in which students tested whether a textbook provided adequate answers to questions they have posed as important. The knowledge that information is so plentifully available in reference works is another argument that classroom time can be spent overcoming other kinds of obstacles.

I am not a panacea giver, and all of this seems difficult to achieve. Sometimes I cannot get beyond giving the students the basic body of information. But I keep trying to establish what I call the pluralist classroom—for them, and for myself. When it works, they are learning because I am learning. At worst, we all make some marginal gains part of the time.

It can sometimes seem discouraging—only two and one half percent a year intellectual growth; severe intellectual depression in the two o'clock class; trying for gain but blaming the students and getting defensive; three students I think are really getting the idea; cannot think of any good exercises and realize that I am not thinking or reading critically myself; when a student made a suggestion, wanted to put him down; when a student asked a question, said to myself, "I hope I can handle this"—defensive, afraid of loss of authority.

But we can in our classrooms just chip away at all these problems, little by little. The teachers are also students and the students are also teachers. If I can remember that. . . .

For a teacher to purvey merely a straight, factual, narrative, 'chronological' history seems to me a trivial task. Books can do that; students can get the information for themselves. For we as teachers to rest content with that level of historical knowledge for students does not, it seems to me, justify our careers, our salaries, our tenure. Nor is merely that level a sufficient foundation for the citizenry of a democracy. That is why I believe the 'chronological history' reformers are selling our students very seriously short.

Teachers need to do more. I have been trying to define what that more might be in the direction of teaching critical skills. I have to add, however, if I believe in the pluralism I have been preaching, that there is no one formula for every teacher or for every group of students.

Coming, as they do, from a variety of backgrounds, students will not go away with one single, uniform, imposed version of history. Some believe that such a uniformity is needed in education to hold society together. But it simply cannot be imposed. What I offer instead is a single conversation about that history and the varied ways it can be interpreted and used.

If you disagree with everything I have said, it is still possible that you now know more about what you think than you did before. You might not have known what you disagreed with unless I had said it. In turn, if I learn about the basis for your disagreement, I may then either modify my opinions or think of a further answer, by which my own formulation of a problem can be extended and reinforced. And that is the point of it all, I believe. It is a quest for Gandhian truth and it is never ended while we live.

In the pluralist classroom, then, students will not gain a final, definitive knowledge of any subject of history, even though they will have acquired a lot of information. During a course, I think the teacher is playing the history to the students and the students learn to play it back, but not just as an echo. The techniques of the play are reading, thinking, writing, and discussion. We learn the information because it was important to the playing, to the discussion and argument. The exercise for both teacher and students leads to better reading, writing, thinking, and argument, and, for the best students, the process will not stop just because the course is over. It becomes part of their lives.

I do not expect such teaching by itself to make the world better, but if some students become a little better able to understand the world we have, that would be a significant achievement.

NOTE

1. From *The Center of Attention,* © 1974 by Daniel Hoffman. New York: Random House, 1974. Used by permission of the author.

15

The Rules of Discussion

A steep slope
of language
                    zigzags
from me to you.

You will break
your neck on it.

You know exactly
what you have said.

            You do not
know what I have heard.

Shirley Kaufman, "After the Voices," *Gold Country*.[1]

To teach these controversial subjects to the diverse student body on today's campuses is difficult. It seems that without some clear rules, rules adhered to by the teacher, accepted by the student audience, and supported by administrations, the task could become impossible.

This chapter title may imply that what follows is such a code, designed to resolve the tensions and dilemmas teachers confront in today's classroom. But I have been unable to come up with such a document, and, on balance, I believe that this is a fortunate failure. A list of rules to be enforced might well have the effect of damping down the flow of free discussion on controversial topics, forcing participants to meander in euphemism and vacuity, lest they call the sanctions of enforcement down upon themselves. Yet, if I cannot come up with clear rules, what redress can I offer against demeaning or insulting language? What follows is a kind of map of the points where conflict and misunderstanding might occur. I am especially interested here in the campus forums and classrooms where controversial issues are discussed rather than in the campus as a whole. My discussion is founded on the assumption, as I have stated before, that liberty is the surest basis for pluralism.

One guideline at least we can agree on: ethnic slurs and racial insults are a breach of the rules of discussion. Ridding the academic classroom and forum of these would seem to be an essential first step in establishing conditions for the free discussion of sensitive issues—but only a first step. So far, most deliberations of these issues have only gone this far, and the grave problem remains of defining the offense. The task is not as easy at it seems.

For a start, all participants must distinguish between illustrative quotations and the personal views of participants. The language of prejudice will have to be used in order for issues pertaining to that language to be freely taught and openly debated. Whatever sensitivities may exist in the audience, the presence of the offending language is not, therefore, itself a breach of the rules.

As a second rule, we might agree that personal or *ad hominem* attacks on individuals break the rules. Again, there are formidable obstacles to definition and enforcement. Good academic discussion can become heated, and feelings can become ruffled. A person may well feel that his or her dignity, identity, and self have been attacked, not simply his or her views and beliefs. But it is a lively discussion. Rather than cry foul or respond in kind, it is better to pause in the discussion of the issues and spend some time discussing the discussion. Here it can be noted that ad hominem arguments are the weakest possible arguments in discussion. They are in fact weak to the point of being selfdiscrediting. Has an ad hominem argument really been used, or not? If so, the user has just lost the argument. The victim of the attack may wish to point this out rather than responding in kind or trying to punish the breach of rules.

What about a rule that all controversial presentations must be *balanced*? This is a very tempting and seemingly harmless rule. It is one that I cannot accept, and my objections come from two directions. One is that a predefined balance restricts the discussion to one axis, either/or, as if there were only two sides to any question. Something is always left out. An argument may come from left field, but that should still be part of the ball park. In discussions that are multidimensional, without preconceived rules about what is admissible, participants stand the best chance of learning something new.

Also, it seems to me that the one-sided presentation of a point of view is a valuable pedagogical method. Only forcing students to agree with the viewpoint, under threat of getting a lower grade, would be a breach of the rules. The point is easier to see in terms of assigned course reading. A textbook may be more than a quarry of information covering a subject—and the assumption that this is the only role of textbooks and lectures is the source of a lot of the misunderstanding of the issue of balance. The textbook may also be a document for discussion. A textbook containing extreme views the audience disagrees with may, indeed, stimulate more thought than one that confirms the views of the readers. The task both of readers of a biased text and auditors of a biased lecture is not to be offended but to test their own opinions against the contrary ones placed before them. Reading what you disagree with is an important way of learning.

The great merit of hearing a convinced and articulate expression of a point of view you disagree with is the possibility of sharpening and strengthening your own attitudes. The most effective argument for any case will incorporate and give full consideration to the best available counter-evidence against that case. To consider such evidence, no matter how personally odious the process, is, in fact, the only way to achieve the ability to convince someone not convinced by your position already.

The auditor or reader receiving a biased presentation therefore has some interesting critical tasks—thinking through the arguments for the case, and then marshalling the counter-arguments, and these are often implicit in the one-sided book or lecture.

A requirement that presentations be balanced, then, does not work as an enforceable guideline. What is the unit of balance anyway? Each lecture, each course, or each educational program? In a one-sided presentation, I would argue, each participant provides his/her own balance.

This argument that a one-sided, unbalanced presentation is in a sense self-correcting is well illustrated in the case of examinations. Examinations are not only to evaluate students' performances but are a valuable learning device. One very common examination technique in the social sciences is the presentation of controversial assertions, to which examinees must respond. It cannot be presumed that the instructor agrees with the assertions contained in the questions; nor are students required to agree with them. The ability of examinees to use their knowledge to respond to such assertions and make their own arguments—rather than simply reciting facts—is an important part of what students should have learned in any course dealing with these world controversies.

I would here like to turn the whole issue of a possible set of 'rules of discussion' on its head. I would suggest that being offended by language you disapprove of when no one has attacked you personally is one possible way that the rules might be broken. This is, in fact, now one of the commonest ways that free discussion is stifled. The 'being offended' trigger has at times been so sensitive that open discussion of some issues before a general audience has become next to impossible. If free academic discussion is to be maintained, we truly need more patience on this score.

Besides the perceived presence of racist or slurring language, ad hominem attacks, or biased presentations, which sometimes trip the 'being offended' trigger, two other issues need discussion in this context: the 'invidious comparison' and the claim of some members of certain communities that insiders have a monopoly of valid knowledge about the community.

Some comparisons are almost automatically insulting to one (or both) of the groups being compared. Yet I am at first inclined to state that no comparison is, *in itself*, a breach of the rules of discussion. But I need to be cautious here. It is certainly possible to pose comparisons whose main purpose is to cause offense.

Clearly, comparison is a difficult aspect of this discussion. The purpose for which a comparison is made, and the method by which it is constructed, are both important in judging the fairness and acceptability of any given example. Comparison is not the listing of similarities but the analysis of differences within a common category. To compare is not to arrive at the same answers but to ask the same set of questions—whether the answers are the same or not is the purpose of the comparison to find out. Therefore, to assert that two cases of something are 'not comparable' is to presume to know the answers without making the inquiry at all. And it is the purpose of academic discussion to inquire. 'You cannot make such a comparison without insulting me' is one path to stifling academic discussion.

But it is vitally important that the comparison be constructed as an inquiry and not as a listing of similarities. The person making the comparison must first establish the larger common category which comprises the specific cases, and must then proceed with a set of analytical questions to be applied to each. This is not easy, and the appropriateness and intellectual value of any given comparison might well be, ought to be, the subject of vigorous methodological debate. But the debate should be free of ad hominem accusations of bad faith. My bias on this difficult issue is that many people have been too quickly offended by given comparisons. It is a fine and controversial line that must be drawn here.

On the question of offense taken because 'others' are making statements and presuming they have knowledge about one's community, I will state my rule with somewhat more confidence: No community is privileged with the exclusive right to make statements about itself. Everyone whatever can discuss the affairs of any community. The idea that only *we* can make valid statements about them is unacceptable in academic discussion.

The insiders of any community may indeed have special knowledge and insight about themselves. But the outsiders' right to discuss the matter from their own perspective is simply undeniable. And in free academic discussion, the difference of perspective between insiders and outsiders ought to be a source of mutual learning and mutual interest. It is the purpose of academic discussion to break down such barriers—not necessarily to achieve agreement: clearer and better understood disagreement will do as well.

Do those making claims that members of their community have the exclusive right to speak about themselves ever give up the claim to valid knowledge about other communities? Not to my knowledge. This test of reversibility shows why claims of this exclusive right are the death of academic discussion. Carried to its logical conclusion, the doctrine would rule out all general discussion of human affairs.

A knotty question of academic freedom arises when professors make controversial statements on subjects outside their field of research expertise. Such statements are often counted as an irresponsible abuse of academic freedom. But this kind of accusation assumes that professorial statements must be authoritatively based on research expertise, so that, in effect, the academic freedom to make statements would be more limited than the equivalent general freedom of speech rights held by all citizens.

That limit is unacceptable. It would place truly suffocating restraints on free academic discussion. Professors are teaching general courses, in which a great variety of matters will be discussed, a great many connections made, sometimes in the spontaneous flow of discussion. Each course has a defined subject matter, but that may not be the most important aspect of what students are learning. It is not a body of 'scientifically established' information being taught in the social sciences. To me, that is a positivist delusion. The ability to carry on a freewheeling discussion of controversial questions, the willingness to learn from those one disagrees with (which need not involve giving up your own convictions)—these values are what professors are teaching as much as a body of information about a subject.

In making the foregoing points, I have not referred to any community or to any particular conflict. What I am talking about are conflicts of the contemporary world in which, quite possibly, people are killing each other and in which members of the academic audience have deeply felt convictions and loyalties. I am saying that in the academic environment, we must preserve the ability to discuss all sides of any such question without recriminations and accusations of bad faith. That is asking a lot, and I intend to ask a lot. The ability to apply cool thought to hot issues is one of the things that higher education at its best ought to be able to offer to society.

I do not wish to make light of anyone who feels offended, hurt, or insulted by the things that may be said in an academic discussion. Their concerns and feelings are real. And I am conscious that in treating these issues I have not provided a set of enforceable rules. What can we do to preserve and enhance the quality of academic discussion? For myself, as things stand, there are half a dozen controversies in the world I will bring up only with the greatest trepidation, even when they are clearly relevant to my presentation.

I believe I have come up with something of value here. It is simply this. When things get too heated and accusations are flying back and forth . . . pause; shift the focus: discuss the discussion.

The freedom to discuss is a high value. If academics are too timid, too inclined to back away from all controversy, then academic freedom may slip away very quietly without anyone even realizing it for a long time. And academic freedom is not a kind of luxurious professorial immunity. It is an aspect of general social freedom. It is the context in which general social freedom can be intensively used and tested, so that it is kept fresh and active, so that it is there when it is needed.

What I recommend, in short, are the courage to speak and the patience to listen. If we do not have both, we will not have either. Those who feel offended by something they have heard should at least pause to consider that language is difficult, misunderstanding easy, disagreement inevitable in human affairs, and free debate vital in a democracy.

NOTE

1. From *Gold Country* by Shirley Kaufman, published by University of Pittsburgh Press, 1973, © Shirley Kaufman. Used by permission of the author.

16

In Pursuit of Pluralism

Praise then
The arts of law and science as of life
The arts of sound and substance as of faith
Which claim us here
To take, as a building, as a fiction, takes us,
Into another frame of space
Where we can ponder, celebrate, and reshape
Not only what we are, where we are from,
But what in the risk and moment of our day
We may become.

Josephine Miles, "Center," *Collected Poems*.[1]

Chapter 1 set down ambitious goals for an education in pluralism, ones manifestly difficult to achieve: the fostering of citizens knowledgeable about the world, sensitive to the dilemmas of reconciling liberty and justice, and accustomed to discussing controversial issues. Students with these values and skills would help to overcome conflict, maintain harmony, open opportunities, and achieve justice in society. These are tall orders for one classroom.

Indeed, later chapters set a more pessimistic, or realistic tone, with no claims of easy miracles, but only partial, inconsistent, incremental gains. My ventures in comparative analysis, for example, would only help a few students understand some historical situations a little better. One classroom, I concluded, could not make the world better but might at least help a few students understand the world we have.

There is no contradiction here. All teachers are familiar with the reality of pursuing lofty goals through limited resources. Of course the results coming from one classroom are going to be small.

And my personal claim is not that I am some sort of unique and extraordinary teacher but only that I have thought about these problems.

One of my conclusions is that these small ways by which classroom give and take and free discussion may serve to extend sympathies, arouse curiosity, and shift attitudes are simply the best means for pursuing pluralism in education—gradual, slight, and inconsistent as their impact is. It will, of course, take thousands, tens of thousands of classrooms, at all levels of education, to accomplish even a small part of what is needed—and teachers, teachers in these classrooms.

This emphasis on the role of teachers is worth underscoring. Some believe, it seems, that teaching through the computer might provide some kind of magic solution, as an alternative to actual teachers in classrooms. Having students learn to use computers is undoubtedly important, but it will be a mistake to think that computers could ever replace the interaction of teachers and students. One thing computers do well is to provide access to more information, and information is not what is lacking. Again, in common systems of computer learning, the program sets a series of questions, with students proceeding through the lesson by choosing correct answers. Yet how can such systems serve for subjects in which, as Robert Brentano wrote, there are no real answers? And how will students learn the empowering skill of asking their own questions?

The idea that computers can take a major role in teaching students stems from the 'positivist' bias discussed in earlier chapters, the belief that imparting large bodies of straight information, and getting students to give correct answers, are the main business of education. The argument of chapter 14 about the place of facts bears repetition here: facts are only the starting point of education; they are for use and are not simply something to possess.

Another reason I have stressed modest goals and low expectations is that high expectations are dangerous. Over and over in American history, when reformers have launched ambitious projects, they count on major changes to come within a couple of years, or even within a few months. The result in our history has often been that disillusionment sets in, and useful ongoing processes are then scuttled and wrecked.

A third point about the need for teachers in classrooms addressing the problems of pluralism: education cannot solve these problems by itself. Too much is asked of schools in dealing with our social problems. Other institutions need to be involved, other commitments made. I leave it to others to expand this point.

With these general points in mind, I can now proceed to summarize what I hope to accomplish in my one classroom, in which I teach students courses in South African and general African history, and the history of European imperialism and expansion around the globe in modern times.

I hope *not* to become embroiled in the shrill, destructive, even dangerous series of accusations and counteraccusations about pluralism, multi-culturalism, political correctness and 'the Canon'.

I hope to protect my calling against the attacks made on it by visible and powerful politicians, attacks which could lead to devastating harm to our fragile and valuable institutions of higher education.

And, most importantly, my hope, naturally, is to influence the students I teach. Since I teach many students who will become teachers, and many more who are already in teaching jobs, I even hope for some kind of multiplier effect. But I do not expect or even desire that my students should adopt all my ideas about how to teach and what should be taught. The tens of thousands of classroom that will contribute to our society's education in pluralism, including the few I might influence, will all be different from each other, and that is as it should be. These differences are one aspect of the pluralism we are working for.

In these varied classrooms, there are two aspects of diversity, discussed at length in previous chapters. One is the diversity of the student body itself, diversity in ethnic and racial identity, cultural background, and religious and political commitments. The other aspect of diversity is in the curriculum, in the material studied. The particular subjects I teach have enabled me to illustrate from my own classroom how the diverse subject matter and the diverse audience could interact to provide an education in pluralism.

What I have attempted to show is how students can be drawn into a single conversation about controversial issues without undue conflict or enforced conformity. To accomplish this, my first task, as recounted in chapter 4, is to break down the claims of some communities that their own affairs are a privileged preserve, which others cannot enter. I criticize, too, the several widespread and longterm student biases, biases held in common by students of various backgrounds. These are, especially, their cultural relativism, a positivist preference for facts, and often an uncritical sympathy for certain Third World revolutionary perspectives. Neither in my classes nor, I hope, in this book, do I wish to *attack* students or disparage them. A teacher's task is to have conversations with them, in which they will need to defend and articulate their beliefs, testing them against a wide variety of evidence and opposing beliefs.

The approach by which I offer students a variety of partial perspectives I call Gandhian truth. It is based on Gandhi's belief that Truth in an absolute sense does exist but is not accessible to human beings. All we can hope for, in this approach, is a partial, lowercase truth, and none of us, therefore, is on sure enough ground to punish others for 'heresy', or to refuse to consider another's perspective. In chapter 3 and, I hope, throughout the book, I showed that this approach had a number of advantages over the widely fashionable cultural relativism most students come in with.

In courses about our pluralist world, the problem of 'the Other' is a key one. The relativist, I have argued, is mainly concerned to avoid ethnocentrism and to be tolerant of differing customs and cultures. The Gandhian engagement with the differing customs and cultures she encounters leads to very different results, ones in which 'otherness' can be broken down so that she—and all of us—may come to a greater awareness of the common humanity of peoples of varying backgrounds. This process of expanding awareness can come into play within the diverse student audience and in our study of other regions of the world. This kind of interchange, with other students, with other cultures being studied, has greater rewards in real understanding of the world and a feeling of kinship with it, and it also brings greater risks of classroom confrontations.

The goal of this kind of teaching is similar to what Richard Rorty has called *solidarity*:

> Solidarity. . . is created by increasing our sensitivity to the particular details of the pain and humiliation of other, unfamiliar sorts of people. Such increased sensitivity makes it more difficult to marginalize people different from ourselves by thinking, 'They do not feel it as *we* would,' or 'There must always be suffering, so why not let *them* suffer?' (*Contingency, Irony, and Solidarity*, p. xvi)

This is a difficult message to put across in our society. It is not bigotry but often simple complacency that stands in the way. I noted to an adult evening class a television news program I had seen a couple of years ago. It was Thanksgiving, and the reporter asked a series of people in New York what they were thankful for. Seven in a row said, "My health!" I exclaimed that no one had said, "My freedom." All of the students disagreed. Their freedom, they said, could be taken for granted; they never thought about it. "My health is the only thing," said one, and that seemed to be the general view.

Caring for one's health is surely laudable. But such a single-minded focus is a symptom of a deeper problem, one of the health of our society. More and more in my classes, it is not overt racism I encounter but something much more subtle. It is a self-centeredness that may imply indifference to the problems of justice in a pluralist society. It is a certain complacency and 'fear of falling,' disguised by the students' relativism and by their commonly held 'liberalism of distant issues'. I hope my efforts as a teacher can help students examine these attitudes. That is the kind of influence I would like to have.

There are secret weapons to aid in fostering this kind of concern for others. They provide the best hope that students will continue the pursuit of pluralism after they have left my class. I am not talking about computers, but about books.

The reading skills of American college students and their interest in reading are widely discerned as one of the serious problems of American education. I occasionally get a student who has slipped through and really cannot read very well. I am not able to comment on that aspect of the problem. Most students can read well enough but are not much in the habit of reading serious literature on their own. To get students interested in reading, to hook them, so that they will read even beyond course assignments, is one of my main goals in teaching.

The standard writing assignment in any of my courses is to have students read a couple of books—novels, stories, memoirs, or essays—from the regions being studied, and to respond with an essay. It is not a "term paper" in which they can simply look up information. They must comment on the books, and they are on their own. I tell them that no one in all time has ever written an essay on this particular material. This statement may even be true in some cases.

My purpose in making such assignments is to open up the rich, largely unfamiliar stores of literature from across the world. Another unacknowledged purpose is to lure some of the students into the reading habit. No sources are more effective than these in giving access to others' lives and cultures.

In these last years of the twentieth century, an abundance of literary wealth comes to us from all over the world. Seeking it out, discovering new authors, is one of my great pleasures.

A few examples will serve to illustrate the literary wealth I am talking about. New Zealand literature is a good place to start: The rich and extravagant language of Keri Hulm in *The Bone People* is riveting; my personal regret is that I do not have it still to read. From Nigeria, Wole Soyinka's boyhood experiences in *Ake* are painfully vivid and beautiful. The hero of the book, in some ways, is the school principal Ransome Kuti, and one must reflect that his wise and humane teaching of courage and integrity was too much for the Nigeria of the 1970s, where such qualities may have helped his protégés to imprisonment and torture. Comparable reflections come, too, from J. M. Coetzee's *Life and Times of Michael K*, and I can sympathize with the student whose paper on this book was two years late. He had only five pages and he wanted to plumb the book's ultimate meaning. He could not write the paper—for the same reasons that I could not genuinely grade it. Coetzee's subsequent books, *Foe* and *Age of Iron*, are profound parables of cultural contact and of the social disintegration of late Apartheid.

In other courses, I might list books by Amitav Ghosh, Neil Bisoondath, Caryl Phillips. These writers, different as they are from each other, all reveal a new, cosmopolitan, post-colonial world of immigrants and emigrants, as the settings and characters in their stories and novels move from Calcutta to London, from Trinidad to Toronto, or from the Caribbean to Britain. Their books reflect a complex synthesis in which colonial and traditional influences are intricately combined. With a sudden surge of recognition, I realize that I am seeing the societies and mentalities whose origins I recount in my courses.

The riches of available literature come from so many directions that I can only baldly summarize. The books come not only individually but in series. Virago Books provides me with the autobiography of Storm Jameson, a self-styled minor writer whose life and career were devoted to the problems of freedom, oppression, and conscience in the moral and political chaos of twentieth century Europe. Pantheon Modern Classics yields Yashar Kemal's epic of Turkish bandit life, and in Oxford's Twentieth Century Classics we find *The Village in the Jungle*, one of the great classics of Sri Lankan literature—written by the former colonial officer Leonard Woolf. And the vast African Writers Series offers so much—Chinua Achebe, Ngugi waThiongo, Stanlake Samkange—but what sticks in my mind is how in *An Egyptian Childhood* the young Taha Husein, having memorized the Koran, could not recite to his father. The universal qualities of family and childhood are here vividly portrayed across decades, across languages, across cultures.

Other long time favorites I am waiting for, hoping and believing that more books will come from them. I wonder what totally original theme Brian Moore will find. I try to imagine how V. S. Naipaul can pierce through the hypocrisies of our world more deftly than he already has. I wait eagerly, too, for another book by Margaret Drabble, an author who probes deeply the conflicted social values of post-imperial British society. For other topics, I might turn to Anita Desai, Nadine Gordimer, Mario Vargas Llosa, or Milan Kundera, who reminds us how tenuous is the freedom to write and to read, how difficult the fight to preserve it.

And these are only a few samples of the rich literature now available and the varied, pluralist world it opens up. That such a wide variety of books and authors is accessible for my courses is a function of the freedom and wealth of our society. They offer a chance for students to engage in the most exciting pursuit of pluralism.

To read such literature is not just entertainment. Over and over, these writings carry warnings of the dangers we are in, and for some authors, writing at all is an act of courage. All of these writers are warning us in one way or another that freedom is fragile, justice difficult to achieve and maintain, civilization threatened. Their moving depictions of common humanity and its predicaments, from other lands, from other cultures, from other times, are valuable reminders lest, in complacency or political excitement, we forget. The need for a tolerance of differences and disagreements seems to me all the greater in the United States, because established and affluent classes of Americans have more power than is good for people. The unique ability of books to expand the relatively narrow confines of individual experience is the message I wish to get across, and too many of our society see no need to bother.

In his book *In My Father's House*, the Ghanaian scholar Kwame Anthony Appiah, now teaching in the United States, gives similar reasons for the inclusion of African literature in American curricula:

> In the American academy, on the other hand, the reading of African writing is reasonably directed by other purposes: by the urge to continue the repudiation of racism; by the need to extend the American imagination— an imagination that regulates much of the world system economically and politically—beyond the narrow scope of the United States; by the desire to develop views of the world elsewhere that respect more deeply the autonomy of the Other, views that are not generated by the local political needs of America's multiple diasporas. (p. 70)

The dangers we are in—not to speak of those that threaten the very survival of humankind, though these are enough, and the entire system could end tomorrow—stem from complacency and intolerance. The great wealth of literature so readily available for course assignments can only act against these vices if people read. If we are not exposed to such literature, what will keep us from being complacent about the sufferings of others? Or from reacting with fear rather than compassion toward those who have less?

Without such reading, too, many might be complacent about the climate of liberty in which alone our diverse society can flourish. The cultural and political conditions in which free writing, bookselling, reading, and teaching can be done are fragile. That these matters seem of less concern to those not involved with books is part of the problem. Our freedom is held in common, and we stand or fall together.

Kurt Vonnegut Jr. recounted how he wanted to influence Congressmen, Senators, and Statesmen, but saw no way at first to gain the attention of such preoccupied and busy people. Then he realized that he could reach them in their college years, before they became powerful. His books could then "poison their minds with humanity." It is a lot to ask of books, but there is little else to turn to for the task. And Vonnegut's strategy requires the freedom to write, to publish, to read, to choose, to debate (Mahoney, *Tropic Miami Herald Sunday Magazine*, January 24, 1971, 8–10, 13, 44).

Andre Brink, Milan Kundera, and Ngugi wa-Thiongo have had to fight for this freedom, the same freedom that gives me access to this comstock lode of worldwide cultural wealth. In some places it is tenuous, in some places it does not exist; is such freedom safe even here? With deep shame and embarrassment, I note that Llosa, Fuentes, Dario Fo, and many other distinguished writers have in the past been denied free entry into the United States but have had to make special application for visas. This is their punishment for their unwillingness to be sycophantic yes-men to American foreign policy. An entire country can be punished, too, as in the proposals of a few years ago to restrict trade with New Zealand, whose people had the effrontery to be a democracy rather than a client state. At least our government is not in the book banning business, though one sees notices, almost weekly, of vigilante groups trying to protect their schools and public libraries from books they deem subversive or immoral.

Two images come to mind that drive home for me the power and the value of books: the first from Czechoslovakia, the second from China. Milan Kundera records that when the Soviet tanks rumbled into Prague in 1968, the newly imposed hard line Communist regime moved first against writers and literary magazines. If free cultural expression survived, they knew, the spirit of the people could not be broken. Again, Yang Jiang recounts how she was sent into exile to a remote peasant commune during the Cultural Revolution. In her memoir, *A Cadre School Life* she records with quiet dignity the bleak and often cruel life of political indoctrination and agricultural labor. She survived, and when she and her husband were finally given permission to return to Peking, they pondered whether they would be able to live and survive in this remote spot:

> "If we had a little hut like this one we could settle down here, couldn't we?"
> He thought it over for a moment and replied dolefully, "We don't have any books."
> He was right. We could do without every other type of material comfort, but without books, life would be impossible. (p. 88)

In recent semesters, I have gone beyond my standard outside reading essay assignment. For some of my classes, I have distributed a kind of international list of novels, memoirs, and essays, books the class is not required to read. On two or three recent occasions, former students meeting me some time after they had completed my class have told me, "I read some of those books." With so much going on nowadays to dissuade students from reading books, I could only feel a sense of triumph.

For the best students, I argued at the end of chapter 14, the process does not stop just because a course is over. It becomes part of their lives. That is my best hope.

When I consider what higher education might do to advance the goals of liberty, justice, and enlightenment in American society— for that is what an education in pluralism ought to represent—I think of how effectively Josephine Miles pursued these goals at Berkeley during her career. I have quoted her poems about teaching and learning throughout this book.

> . . .
> I see her sitting, talking
>   books piled around her
> (no one laughs harder amidst the pyramid of knowledge)
> . . .
> we learn about irony and compassion
>   how to balance laughter and anguish.
> . . .

This from James Schevill's description of her character and influence. ("How Language Spells Us": A Sequence for Josephine Miles, *Ambiguous Dancers of Fame*, 264, 265.[2])

Her career is representative of the host of other men and women of past generations who created and sustained our academic institutions.

Coming after them, our task is, as Rachel Hadas says, to "pass it on." This means not to duplicate our predecessors but to continue to grow and develop as we face the complex problems of higher education in the new century and the new millennium.

NOTES

1. Reprinted from the poem "Center," in the book *Collected Poems, 1930–83* by Josephine Miles. © Josephine Miles 1983. University of Illinois Press. Used by permission of the publisher.

2. Reprinted from the poem "How Language Spells Us: A Sequence for Josephine Miles," in the book *Ambiguous Dancers of Fame*, by James Schevill. © James Schevill 1987. Swallow Press/Ohio University Press. Used by permission of the publisher.

Bibliography

For these essays, I will append a bibliographical list for each chapter or pair of closely related chapters. The essays are not research pieces, and the books listed are not the sources of the essays, though some of the books listed molded my thinking in these matters. The books included on the list are selective and perhaps at times arbitrary. In some cases, they have the status of suggestions for further reading. In others, they provide, perhaps, a medium for teachers desiring to try some of the pedagogical approaches discussed in the essays. I have not listed many books about education and I have not used many. That may be my loss. University teachers are seldom taught how to teach. They have to work that out for themselves.

Taken as a whole, this is a varied and perhaps idiosyncratic list. Those books I should not have been bothering with if I were to progress in the narrower research field have often been the most valuable in developing my thinking. The books listed are in many cases ones that I believe made a big difference to me, made me a different person for having read them. The list reflects, too, my habit of developing my views out of readings I disagree with as much, perhaps more, as from readings coinciding with my own views. In some cases, the reading was done a long time ago, in others more recently.

In the rich world of books, with the titles on any one subject itself too large to be covered by one person, there is something to be said for a little haphazard reading. From time to time I encourage some students to sneak off and read something remote from their specialties, if only they can find the time and can overcome being too much dominated by a strictly defined subject area for their forthcoming oral examinations.

Chapter 1 One Classroom: An Introduction

These are the key works of the debates on the curriculum, the canon, multiculturalism, and political correctness, with some of the ongoing commentary from periodicals.

Aufderheide, Patricia, ed. *Beyond P. C.: Toward a Politics of Understanding.* St. Paul: Graywolf Press, 1992.

Berman, Paul, ed. *Debating P. C.: The Controversy over Political Correctness on College Campuses.* New York: Laurel, 1992.

Bloom, Allan. *The Closing of the American Mind.* New York: Simon & Schuster, 1987.

Curtin, Philip D. "Depth, Span, and Relevance," *American Historical Review.* 89, (February 1984), 1–9.

Dahl, Robert A. *A Preface to Democratic Theory.* Chicago: University of Chicago Press, 1956.

D'Souza, Dinesh. *Illiberal Education: The Politics of Race and Sex on Campus.* New York: The Free Press, 1991.

Fredrickson, George M. "No Foreigners Need Apply," *New York Times Book Review*, August 22, 1993, 17.

Gless, Darryl J. and Barbara Herrnstein Smith, eds. *The Politics of Liberal Education.* Durham: Duke University Press, 1991.

Hirsch, E. D., Jr. *Cultural Literacy.* Boston: Houghton Mifflin Co., 1987.

Hirsch, E. D. Jr. et al. *The Dictionary of Cultural Literacy.* New York: Houghton Mifflin Co., 1988.

Hook, Sidney. "The Closing of the American Mind: An Intellectual Best-Seller Revisited," *The American Scholar* 58. No. 1 (Winter 1989): 123–35.

Miles, Josephine. *Collected Poems.* Champaign: University of Illinois Press, 1983.

Naipaul, V. S. "Our Universal Civilization." *New York Review of Books* 38, No. 6 (January 31, 1991): 22–25.

The New Republic, February 18, 1991.

Simonson, Rich and Scott Walker, eds. *The Graywolf Annual Five: Multicultural Literacy.* St. Paul: Graywolf Press, 1988.

Chapter 2 Conflicting Views of the Classroom Revolution

Here I will cite works by Agard, Brentano, and Curtin. These are not complete bibliographies but works that best illustrate their qualities as teachers.

Agard, Walter R. *What Democracy Meant to the Greeks*. Madison: University of Wisconsin Press, 1960.

_____. "Classics on the Midwestern Frontier." In *The Frontier in Perspective*, edited by Wyman and Kroeber. Madison: University of Wisconsin Press, 1965.

Becker, Carl L., *Everyman His Own Historian: Essays on History and Politics*. Chicago: Quadrangle Paperbacks, 1966.

Brentano, Robert J. "Bishops and Saints." In *The Historian's Workshop: Original Essays by Sixteen Historians*, edited by L. P. Curtis, Jr. New York: Alfred A. Knopf, 1970, pp. 23–45.

_____. *Two Churches: England and Italy in the Thirteenth Century*. Princeton: Princeton University Press, 1968.

Curtin, Philip D. "The Lure of Bambuk Gold." *The Journal of African History*. 14, no. 4 (1973): 623–631.

_____. *Cross-Cultural Trade in World History*. Cambridge: Cambridge University Press, 1984.

_____. "Depth, Span, and Relevance." *American Historical Review* 89 (February 1984): 1–9.

_____. "Graduate Teaching in World History." *Journal of World History*. 2, no. 1 (Spring 1991): 81–89.

Hancock, W. K. *Survey of British Commonwealth Affairs: volume II: Problems of Economic Policy, 1918–1939. Part 2*. London: Oxford University press, 1940 (reprinted 1964).

Meiklejohn, Alexander. *The Experimental College*, edited and abridged by John Walker Powell. Cabin John: Seven Locks Press, 1981.

Chapter 3 The Teacher's Pitch and the Student Audience

The list for this essay pertains not to the pedagogical problems I discuss. I cite instead the discussions of Gandhi's life and thought that I have found most compelling and important. In addition, the books listed on colonialism and imperialism have been important for me far beyond their specific subject areas. The republication of Cohn's articles in book form reveals one of my secrets. The essay itself stems from such readings as these in an indirect way. How, I asked myself, could I put over this kind of analysis in a way that students would understand?

On Gandhi:

Bondurant, Joan. *Conquest of Violence: The Gandhian Philosophy of Conflict.* rev. ed. Berkeley: University of California Press, 1965.

Borman, William. *Gandhi and Non-Violence.* Albany: State University of New York Press, 1986.

Brown, Judith. *Gandhi: Prisoner of Hope.* New Haven: Yale University Press, 1989.

Erikson, Erik. *Gandhi's Truth: On the Roots of Militant Non-Violence.* New York: Norton, 1969.

Gandhi, M. K. *An Autobiography: the Story of My Experiments with Truth.* Boston: Beacon Press, 1957.

Rudolph, Lloyd I. and Suzanne. *Gandhi: The Traditional Roots of Charisma.* Chicago: University of Chicago Press, 1983.

On colonial history:

Cohn, Bernard S. *An Anthropologist among the Historians and Other Essays.* Delhi: Oxford University Press, 1990.

France, Peter. *The Charter of the Land: Custom and Colonization in Fiji.* Melbourne: Oxford University Press, 1969.

Hutchins, Francis. *The Illusion of Permanence: British Imperialism in India.* Princeton: Princeton University Press, 1967.

Low, D. A. *Lion Rampant: Essays in the Study of British Imperialism.* London: Frank Cass, 1973.

Chapter 4 Insiders and Outsiders

Some of these works deal with the issue of insider and outsider; others are criticisms of the arrogance and limitation of outsider attempts to understand. Still others claim some special insider advantage. See also readings for chapter 12 below for some different aspects of this issue:

Amin, Samir, *Eurocentrism.* New York: Monthly Review Press, 1989.

Asad, Talal, ed. *Anthropology and the Colonial Encounter.* London: Ithaca Press, 1973.

Asante, Molefi Kete. *Afrocentricity.* Trenton: African World Press, 1988.

Berkhofer, Robert J. Jr. *The White Man's Indian: Images of the American Indian from Columbus to the Present.* New York: Vintage Books, 1979.

Clifford, James. *The Predicament of Culture: Twentieth Century Ethnography, Literature, and Art.* Cambridge: Harvard University Press, 1988.

Dumas, Henry. *Knees of a Natural Man.* New York: Thunder's Mouth Press, 1989.

Geertz, Clifford. *Works and Lives: the Anthropologist as Author.* Stanford: Stanford University Press, 1988.

Gilsenan, Michael. *Recognizing Islam: Religion and Society in the Modern Arab World.* New York: Pantheon Books, 1982.

Goitein, S. D. *Jews and Arabs: Their Contacts through the Ages, 3rd ed.* New York: Schocken Books, 1974.

Horton, Robin. "African Traditional Thought and Western Science." *Africa* (1967); 50–71, 155–87.

Kabbani, Rana. *Europe's Myths of Orient.* Bloomington: Indiana University Press, 1986.

Kincaid, Jamaica. *A Small Place.* New York: New American Library, 1989.

Leed, Eric J. *The Mind of the Traveler: From Gilgamesh to Global Tourism.* New York, Basic Books, 1991.

Levenson, Joseph R. *Confucian China and Its Modern Fate: A Trilogy.* Berkeley and Los Angeles: University of California Press, 1968.

Lewis, Bernard. "Other People's History." *American Scholar* 59, no. 3 (Summer 1990): 397–405.

MacCannell, Dean. *The Tourist: A New Theory of the Leisure Class.* New York: Shocken Books, 1989.

Mudimbe, V. Y. *The Invention of Africa: Gnosis, Philosophy and the Order of Knowledge.* Bloomington: Indiana University Press, 1988.

Peel, J. D. Y. "Understanding Alien Belief Systems." *British Journal of Sociology.* 20 (1969): 69–84.

Pryce-Jones, David. *The Closed Circle: An Interpretation of the Arabs*. New York: Harper & Row, 1989.

Said, Edward W. *Orientalism*. New York: Vintage Books, 1979.

Soyinka, Wole. *Myth, Literature and the African World*. New York: Cambridge University Press, 1976.

Chapter 5 The Colonizer and the Colonized

Most of these works pertain to the intellectual history of the colonized. They set forth the various strategies the colonized have developed to deal with the situation they are in. Such works have provided me with the raw material that I use in classes on these topics. The debt that some of these authors owe to Joseph Levenson's analysis of Confucian China is clear—or perhaps I imagine it. My own debt to Levenson inevitably informs the reading I give to any of these books.

Abbott, Freeland. *Islam and Pakistan*. Ithaca: Cornell University Press, 1968.

Aziz Ahmad. *Islamic Modernism in India and Pakistan. 1887–1964*. London: Oxford University Press, 1967.

Curtin, Philip. ed. *Africa and the West*. Madison: University of Wisconsin Press, 1972.

Hansen, Emmanuel. *Frantz Fanon: Social and Political Thought*. Ohio State University Press, 1977.

Heimsath, Charles. *Indian Nationalism and Hindu Social Reform*. Princeton: Princeton University Press, 1964.

Hourani, Albert. *Arabic Thought in the Liberal Age, 1798–1939*. London: Oxford University Press, 1970.

July, Robert. *The Origins of Modern African Thought: Its Development in West Africa during the Nineteenth and Twentieth Centuries*. New York: Frederick A. Praeger, 1967.

McCulloch, Jock. *In the Twilight of Revolution: The Political Theory of Amilcar Cabral*. London: Routledge & Kegan Paul, 1983.

Memmi, Albert. *The Colonizer and the Colonized*. New York: The Orion Press, 1965.

Nandy, Ashis. *The Intim ite Enemy: Loss and Recovery of Self Under Colonialism*. Delhi: Oxford University Press, 1983.

Ranger, T.O. "African Reactions to the Imposition of Colonial Rule in East and Central Africa," in *Colonialism in Africa, 1870–1960. Volume I: The History and Politics of Colonialism, 1870–1914*, edited by L.H. Gann and Peter Duigan. Cambridge: At the University press, 1969.

Safran, Nadav. *Egypt in Search of Political Community: An Analysis of the Intellectual and Political Evolution of Egypt, 1804–1952*. Cambridge: Harvard University Press, 1961.

Sharabi, Hisham. *Arab Intellectuals and the West: The Formative Years, 1875–1914*. Baltimore: The Johns Hopkins Press, 1970.

Sivan, Emmanuel. *Radical Islam: Medieval Theology and Modern Politics*. New Haven: Yale University Press, 1985.

Spitzer, Leo. *The Creoles of Sierra Leone: Responses to Colonialism, 1870–1945*. Madison: The University of Wisconsin Press, 1974.

Chapter 6 The Uses of Comparative History

This is a short selection of some of the most ambitious and successful of attempts at 'comparison in the grand manner.' The Bloch essay, as filled out by Sewell's article, provides the starting point for anyone wishing to attempt historical comparisons.

Adas, Michael. *Prophets of Rebellion: Millenarian Protest Movements against the European Colonial Order*. Chapel Hill: The University of North Carolina Press, 1979.

Bloch, Marc. "Toward a Comparative History of European Societies." In *Enterprise and Secular Change*. Frederic C. Lane and Jelle Riemersma, pp. 494–521. London, 1953.

Cell, John W. *The Highest Stage of White Supremacy: The Origins of Segregation in South Africa and the American South*. New York: Cambridge University Press, 1982.

Chalk, Frank and Kurt Jonassohn. *The History and Sociology of Genocide: Analyses and Case Studies*. New Haven: Yale University Press (published in cooperation with the Montreal Institute for Genocide Studies), 1990.

Chaudhuri, K. N. *Asia before Europe: Economy and Civilisation of the Indian Ocean from the Rise of Islam to 1750*. New York: Cambridge University Press, 1990.

Crosby, Alfred W. Jr. *Ecological Imperialism: The Biological Expansion of Europe, 900–1900.* New York: Cambridge University Press, 1986.

Curtin, Philip D. *The Rise and Fall of the Plantation Complex: Essays in Atlantic History.* Cambridge: Cambridge University Press, 1990.

Degler, Carl N. *Neither Black nor White: Slavery and Race Relations in Brazil and the United States.* New York: The Macmillan Company, 1971.

de Kiewiet, C. W. *A History of South Africa: Social and Economic.* London: Oxford University Press, 1941.

Denoon, Donald. *Settler Capitalism: The Dynamics of Dependent Development in the Southern Hemisphere.* Oxford: Clarendon Press. 1983.

Fredrickson, George M. *White Supremacy: A Comparative Study in American and South African History.* New York: Oxford University Press, 1981.

Hamer, David. *New Towns in the New World: Images and Perceptions of the Nineteenth Century Urban Frontier.* New York: Columbia University Press, 1990.

Hancock, Sir Keith. *Survey of British Commonwealth Affairs, 1918–1939. vol. II, part 2: Problems of Economic Policy, 1918–1939,* London: Oxford University Press, 1940 (reprinted, 1964).

Harrison, John F. C. *Quest for the New Moral World: Robert Owen and the Owenites in Britain and America.* New York: Scribner's, 1969.

Kolchin, Peter. *Unfree Labor: American Slavery and Russian Serfdom.* Cambridge: Harvard University Press, 1987.

Kolko, Gabriel. *Confronting the Third World: United States Foreign Policy, 1945–1980.* New York: Pantheon Books, 1988.

Lamar, Howard and Leonard Thompson, eds. *The Frontier in History: North America and Southern Africa Compared.* New Haven: Yale University Press, 1981.

Lipset, Seymour Martin. *Continental Divide: The Values and Institutions of the United States and Canada.* New York: Routledge, 1990.

Sewell, William H. Jr. "Marc Bloch and the Logic of Comparative History." *History and Theory.* 6, no. 2 (1967): 208–218.

Spitzer, Leo. *Lives in Between: Assimilation and Marginality in Austria, Brazil, West Africa, 1780–1945*. New York: Cambridge University Press, 1989.

Chapters 7 and 8 Teaching a Racially Sensitive Subject, and On Understanding the South African Freedom Struggle

This is a rather arbitrary selection of books on South Africa; but the references in these books will lead the reader to everything else.

Barber, James and John Barratt. *South Africa's Foreign Policy: The Search for Status and Security, 1945–1988*. New York: Cambridge University Press, 1990.

Brown, Joshua, Patrick Manning, Karin Shapiro, Jon Wiener (*Radical History Review*), Belinda Bozzoli & Peter Delius (*The History Workshop*), eds., *History from South Africa: Alternative Visions and Practices*, Philadelphia: Temple University Press, 1991.

Davis, Stephen M. *Apartheid's Rebels: Inside South Africa's Hidden War*. New Haven: Yale University Press, 1987.

Elphick, Richard and Hermann Giliomee. *The Shaping of South African Society, 1652–1840*. Middletown: Wesleyan University Press, 1989.

Gerhart, Gail M. *Black Power in South Africa: The Evolution of an Ideology*. Berkeley: University of California Press, 1978.

Giliomee, Hermann and Lawrence Schlemmer. *From Apartheid to Nation-Building: Contemporary South African Debates*. Cape Town: Oxford University Press, 1989.

Greenberg, Stanley B. *Legitimating the Illegitimate: State, Markets and Resistance in South Africa*. Berkeley: University of California Press, 1987.

Johns, Sheridan and R. Hunt Davis Jr., *Mandela, Tambo and the African National Congress: The Struggle against Apartheid, 1948–1990, A Documentary Survey*. New York: Oxford University Press, 1991.

Kivnick, Helen. *Where is the Way: Song and Struggle in South Africa*. New York: Penguin Books, 1990.

Keegan, Tim. *Facing the Storm: Portraits of Black Lives in Rural South Africa*. Athens: Ohio Univesity Press, 1988.

Lelyveld, Joseph. *Move Your Shadow: South Africa Black and White*. New York: Times Books, 1985.

Malan, Rian. *My Traitor's Heart*. New York: Atlantic Monthly Press, 1990.

Marks, Shula. *The Ambiguities of Dependence: Class, Nationalism, and the State in Twentieth-Century Natal*. Baltimore: The Johns Hopkins University Press, 1986.

Meli, Francis. *A History of the ANC: South Africa Belongs to Us*. Bloomington and Indianapolis: Indiana University Press, 1988.

Minter, William. *King Solomon's Mines Revisited: Western Interests and the Burdened History of Southern Africa*. New York: Basic Books, 1986.

Rieff, Philip. *Fellow Teacher/of Culture and Its Second Death*. Chicago: University of Chicago Press, 1985.

Saunders, Christopher. *The Making of the South African Past: Major Historians on Race and Class*. Totowa: Barnes & Noble, 1988.

Smith, Ken. *The Changing Past: Trends in South African Historical Writing*. Athens: Ohio University Press, 1988.

Sparks, Allister. *The Mind of South Africa*. New York: Alfred A. Knopf, 1990.

Thompson, L. M. *A History of South Africa*. New Haven: Yale University Press, 1990.

_____. *The Political Mythology of Apartheid*. New Haven: Yale University Press, 1985.

Chapter 9 Imperialism

Most of the bibliographical entries for the other chapters pertain in one way or another to this vast subject. These are a few additional studies of imperialism. Also included here are sources for some of the case studies used in classes.

Curtin, Philip D. *Death by Migration: Europe's Encounter with the Tropical World in the Nineteenth Century*. New York: Cambridge University Press, 1989.

Darby, Philip. *Three Faces of Imperialism: British and American Approaches to Asia and Africa, 1870–1970*. New Haven: Yale University Press, 1987.

Dewey, Clive and A. G. Hopkins. *The Imperial Impact: Studies in the Economic History of Africa and India*. University of London: The Athlone Press, 1978.

Doyle, Michael W. *Empires*. Ithaca: Cornell University Press, 1986.

Fieldhouse, D. K. *Economics and Empire*. London: Weidenfeld & Nicholson, 1973.

Guha, Ranajit and Gayatri Chakravorty Spivak, eds. *Selected Subaltern Studies*. New York: Oxford University Press, 1988.

Hancock, W. K. *Wealth of Colonies*. Cambridge: at the University Press, 1950.

Jennings, Francis. *The Invasion of America: Indians, Colonialism, and the Cant of Conquest*. Chapel Hill: University of North Carolina Press, 1975.

Kiernan, V. G. *From Conquest to Collapse: European Empires from 1815 to 1960*. New York: Pantheon Books, 1982.

Koebner, Richard and Helmut Schmidt. *Imperialism: The Story and Significance of a Political Word*. Cambridge: at the University Press, 1964.

McNeill, William. *Plagues and Peoples*. New York: Doubleday, 1976.

Orange, Claudia. *The Treaty of Waitangi*. Wellington: Allen & Unwin, 1987.

Owen, Roger and Bob Sutcliffe, eds. *Studies in the Theory of Imperialism*. London: Longman, 1972.

Parsons, Q. N. *The Word of Khama*. Lusaka: The Historical Association of Zambia, 1972.

Patterson, K. David. *Pandemic Influenza, 1700–1900: A Study in Historical Epidemiology*. Totowa: Rowman & Littlefield, 1986.

Robinson, Ronald and John Gallagher, with Alice Denny. *Africa and the Victorians: the Climax of Imperialism in the Dark Continent*. New York: St. Martin's Press, 1961.

Scammel, G. V. *The First Imperial Age: European Overseas Expansion, c. 1400–1715*. London: Unwin Hyman, 1989.

Shineberg, Dorothy, ed. *The Trading Journals of Andrew Cheyne, 1841–1844*. Honolulu: University of Hawaii Press, 1971.

Thomas, Nicholas. *Entangled Objects: Exchange, Material Culture, and Colonialism in the Pacific*. Cambridge: Harvard University press, 1991.

Thornton, A. P. *Doctrines of Imperialism*. New York: John Wiley & Sons, 1965.

Tidrick, Kathryn. *Empire and the English Character*. London: I. B. Taurus, 1992.

Waddell, Hope. *Twenty-nine Years in the West Indies and Central Africa*, 1863, 2nd rev. ed. London: Frank Cass, 1970.

Warren, Bill. *Imperialism: Pioneer of Capitalism*. London: NLB, 1980.

Chapter 10 Nationalism and Racism: The Keywords

These are the works that have influenced my thinking the most in writing this essay.

Anderson, Benedict. *Imagined Communities: Reflections on the Origin and Spread of Nationalism*. London: Verso, 1983.

Banton, Michael. *Race Relations*. New York: Basic Books, 1967.

Chatterjee, Partha. *Nationalist Thought and the Colonial World: a Derivative Discourse*. London: Zed Books, 1986.

Gellner, Ernest. *Nations and Nationalism*. Ithaca: Cornell University Press, 1983.

Isaacs, Harold R. *Idols of the Tribe: Group Identity and Political Change*. Cambridge: Harvard University Press, 1989.

Rex, John. *Race Relations in Sociological Theory*. 2nd ed. London: Routledge & Kegan Paul, 1983.

van den Berghe, Pierre L. *Race and Racism: A Comparative Perspective*. New York: Wiley, 1967.

Williams, Raymond. *Keywords: A Vocabulary of Culture and Society*. rev. ed. New York: Oxford University Press, 1985.

Young, Crawford. *The Politics of Cultural Pluralism*. Madison: The University of Wisconsin Press, 1976.

Chapter 11 Structures of Argument in African History

Some of the books are listed to illustrate the various structures of argument I have set out in the essay, though it must be said that the structures are set down as ideal types and do not always appear in such a pure form. Other works in this list exhibit one or another of the apologetic postures. In addition, some of these items contribute to historiographical discussion in terms related to the ones I have developed in the essay.

Abraham, W. E. *The Mind of Africa*. Chicago: University of Chicago Press, 1966.

Achebe, Chinua. *Christmas in Biafra and Other Poems*. Garden City: Doubleday & Co., 1973.

Alpers, Edward A. "Rethinking African Economic History: A Contribution to the Discussion of the Roots of Underdevelopment." *Ufahamu*. 3, no. 3 (Winter 1973): 97–129.

Austen, Ralph A. *African Economic History: Internal Development and External Dependency*. Portsmouth, N. H.: Heinemann, 1987.

Bernal, Martin. *Black Athena: The Afroasiatic Roots of Classical Civilization. vol I: The Fabrication of Ancient Greece, 1785–1985*. Rutgers University Press, 1987.

Boahen, A. Adu. *African Perspectives on Colonialism*. Baltimore: The Johns Hopkins University Press, 1987.

Césaire, Aimé. *Return to My Native Land*. Harmondsworth: Penguin Books, 1969.

Chinweizu. *The West and the Rest of Us: White Predators, Black Slavers and the African Elite*. New York: Vintage Books, 1975.

Crowder, Michael. *West Africa Under Colonial Rule*. London: Hutchinson, 1968.

Davidson, Basil. *The African Genius: An Introduction to African Cultural and Social History, Boston: Little, Brown, 1969*.

———. *Black Mother: The Years of the African Slave Trade*. Boston: Little, Brown, 1961.

———. *Let Freedom Come: Africa in Modern History*. Boston: Little, Brown, 1978.

———. *The Lost Cities of Africa*. Boston: Little, Brown, 1957.

Dike, K. Onwuka. *Trade and Politics on the Niger Delta: An Introduction to the Economic and Social History of Nigeria*. Oxford: at the Clarendon Press, 1956.

Diop, Cheikh Anta. *The African Origin of Civilization: Myth or Reality.* Westport: Lawrence Hill, 1974.

Drake, St. Clair. *Black Folk Here and There: An Essay in History and Anthropology.* Los Angeles: Center for Afro-American Culture and Society, University of California, 1987.

Fage, John D. *A History of Africa.* New York: Alfred A. Knopf, 1979.

Freund, Bill. *The Making of Contemporary Africa: The Development of African Society since 1800.* Bloomington: Indiana University Press, 1984.

Gann, Lewis and Peter Duignan. *Burden of Empire: An Appraisal of Western Colonialism in Africa South of the Sahara.* New York: Frederick A. Praeger, 1967.

Goody, Jack. *Technology, Tradition, and the State in Africa.* London: Oxford University Press, 1971.

Hopkins, A. G. *An Economic History of West Africa.* New York: Columbia University Press, 1973.

_____. "On Importing Andre Gunder Frank into Africa." *African Economic History Review* 2 (1975): 13–21.

Iliffe, John. *The African Poor: A History.* New York: Cambridge University Press, 1987.

Isichei, Elizabeth. *A History of Nigeria.* London: Longman, 1983.

Lonsdale, John. "The Emergence of African Nations: A Historiographical Analysis" *African Affairs.* 67 (1968): 11–28.

Oliver, Roland and J. D. Fage. *A Short History of Africa.* London: Penguin Books, 1962.

Roberts, Andrew, ed. *The Colonial Moment in Africa: Essays on the Movement of Minds and Materials, 1900–1940.* New York: Cambridge University Press, 1990.

Rodney, Walter. *How Europe Underdeveloped Africa.* London: Bogle L'Ouverture Publications, 1972.

Snowden, Frank M. Jr. *Blacks in Antiquity: Ethiopians in the Greco-Roman Experience.* Cambridge: Harvard University Press, 1970.

Wallerstein, Immanuel. "Dependence in an Interdependent World: the Limited Possibilities of Transformation within the Capitalist World Economy." *African Studies Review* 17, no. 1 (April 1974): 1–26.

_____. "The Rise and Future Demise of the World Capitalist System: Concepts for Comparative Analysis." *Comparative Studies in Society and History* 16 no. 4 (September 1974): 387–415.

Williams, Chancellor. *The Destruction of Black Civilization: Great Issues of a Race from 4500 B. C. to 2000 A. D.*, rev. ed. Chicago: Third World Press, 1976.

Wrigley, C. C. "Historicism in Africa: Slavery and State Formation." *African Affairs*. 70 (1971): 113–124.

Chapter 12 The Other: The Problem of Authenticity

The books I list under this heading are some whose status and significance I would discuss and explore, and also some that are of assistance in defining the general issue of 'the other.'

Brennan, Timothy. *Salman Rushdie and the Third World: Myths of the Nation.* New York: St. Martin's Press, 1989.

Bugul, Ken. *The Abandoned Baobab: The Autobiography of a Senegalese Woman.* Chicago: Lawrence Hill Books, 1991.

Burgos-Debray, Elisabeth, ed. *I, Rigoberta Menchu: An Indian Woman in Guatemala.* New York: Verso, 1983

Chinweizu. *Voices from Twentieth-Century Africa: Griots and Towncriers.* London: Faber & Faber, 1988.

Chipasula, Frank Mkalawile, ed. *When My Brothers Come Home: Poems from Central and Southern Africa.* Middletown: Wesleyan University Press, 1985.

Feierman, Steven. *Peasant Intellectuals: Anthropology and History in Tanzania.* Madison: University of Wisconsin Press, 1990.

Ignatieff, Michael. *The Needs of Strangers.* New York: Penguin Books, 1984.

Jordan, A. C. *Tales from Southern Africa.* Berkeley: University of California Press, 1973.

Keegan, Tim. *Facing the Storm: Portraits of Black Lives in Rural South Africa*. Athens: Ohio University Press, 1988.

Lyman, Christopher M. *The Vanishing Race and Other Illusions: Photographs of Indians by Edward S. Curtis*. New York: Pantheon Books (for the Smithsonian Institution), 1982.

Masani, Zareer. *Indian Tales of the Raj*. Berkeley: University of California Press, 1987.

Miles, Josephine. *Collected Poems*. Champaign: University of Illinois Press, 1983.

Plaatje, Sol. *Mhudi*. Johannesburg: Quagga Press, 1975.

Sahlins, Marshall. *Islands of History*. Chicago: The University of Chicago Press, 1985.

Saitoti, Tepilit Ole. *The Worlds of a Maasai Warrior: An Autobiography*. Berkeley: University of California Press, 1988.

Shava, Piniel Viviri. *A People's Voice: Black South African Writing in the Twentieth Century*. Athens: Ohio University Press, 1989.

Spence, Jonathan A. *The Question of Hu*. New York: Alfred A. Knopf, 1988.

Todorov, Tzvetan. *The Conquest of America: The Question of the Other*. New York: Harper & Row, 1984.

Vail, Leroy and Landeg White. *Power and the Praise Poem: Southern African Voices in History*. Charlottesville: University Press of Virginia, 1991.

Chapters 13 and 14 The World Context of American Pluralism, and Learning in the Pluralist Classroom

The bibliographies for chapters 3 through 12 apply generally to these chapters. For specific points in chapter 13 and 14, see also the following:

Hofstadter, Richard. *The Idea of a Party System: The Rise of Legitimate Opposition in the United States, 1780–1840*. Berkeley: University of California Press, 1970.

Kuper, Leo and M. G. Smith, eds. *Pluralism in Africa*. Berkeley: University of California Press, 1971.

Chapter 15 The Rules of Discussion

The references listed below are not discussions of the problems of discussion as such. They are, rather, works that provide context and indicate the importance of the issues involved. They represent some of the issues that have had most influence on my thinking.

American Association of University Professors. *Policy Documents & Reports, 1984 Edition*. Washington: AAUP, 1984.

Dahl, Robert A. *A Preface to Democratic Theory*. Chicago: University of Chicago Press, 1956.

Demac, Donna. *Liberty Denied: The Current Rise of Censorship in America*. New York: Pen America Center, 1988.

Novick, Peter. *That Noble Dream: the 'Objectivity Question' and the American Historical Profession*. New York: Cambridge University Press, 1988.

Sanders, Jane. *Cold War on the Campus: Academic Freedom at the University of Washington, 1946–1964*. Seattle: University of Washington Press, 1979.

Schrecker, Ellen W. *No Ivory Tower: McCarthyism and the Universities*. New York: Oxford University Press, 1986.

Chapter 16 In Pursuit of Pluralism

Rather than citing only works mentioned in the essay, I here list some of the latest discoveries, and a couple of old favorites. This, and any of the booklists appended for other essays, could be extended indefinitely.

AlGhitani, Gamal. *Zayni Barakat*. New York: Viking, 1988.

Appiah, Kwame Anthony. *In My Father's House: Africa in the Philosophy of Culture*. New York: Oxford University Press, 1992.

Chinodya, Shimmer. *Harvest of Thorns*. London: Heinemann, 1989.

Essop, Ahmed. *Hajji Musa and the Hindu Fire-Walker*. London: Readers International, 1988.

Ghosh, Amitav. *The Shadow Lines*. New York: Penguin Books, 1990.

Hove, Chenjerai. *Bones*. London: Heinemann, 1990.

Hulm, Keri. *The Bone People*. New York: Penguin Books, 1986.

Johnson, Amryl. *Sequins for a Ragged Hem*. London: Virago Press, 1988.

Johnson, Charles. *Middle Passage*. New York: Atheneum, 1990.

Johnson, Colin. *Doctor Wooreddy's Prescription for Enduring the Ending of the World*. New York: Ballantine Books, 1983.

Kundera, Milan. *The Book of Laughter and Forgetting*. New York: Penguin Books, 1981.

Kuzwayo, Ellen. *Call Me Woman*. San Francisco: Spinster/Aunt Lute, 1985.

Mahfouz, Naguib. *Palace Walk* (Cairo Trilogy, I). New York: Doubleday, 1990.

Mahoney, Lawrence. "Poison Their Minds with Humanity," *Tropic: Miami Herald Sunday Magazine*. January 24, 1971, 8–10, 13, 44.

Mashinini, Emma. *Strikes Have Followed Me All My Life: A South African Autobiography*. New York: Routledge, 1991.

Mattera, Don. *Sophiatown: Coming of Age in South Africa*. Boston: Beacon Press, 1987.

Modisane, Bloke. *Blame Me on History*. New York: Simon & Schuster, 1987.

Morgan, Sally. *My Place*. New York: Henry Holt, 1987

Munif, Abdelrahman. *Cities of Salt*. New York: Vintage International, 1989.

Naipaul, V. S. *A House for Mr. Biswas*. New York: Alfred A. Knopf, 1983.

Rorty, Richard. *Contingency, Irony, and Solidarity*. Cambridge: Cambridge University Press, 1989.

Schevill, James. *Ambiguous Dancers of Fame: Collected Poems, 1945–1986*. Athens: Swallow Press/Ohio University Press, 1987.

Suleri, Sara. *Meatless Days*. Chicago: University of Chicago Press, 1989.

Tantri, K'tut. *Revolt in Paradise*. New York: Clarkson N. Potter, 1989.

Tham, Hilary. *Tigerbone Wine (Poems)*. Washington, D. C.: Three Continents Press, 1992.

Yang, Jiang. *A Cadre School Life: Six Chapters*. London: Readers International 1984.

Index

academic freedom, 167, 168, 169
Accuracy in Academia, 8
Achebe, Chinua, 119, 177
activism, 82, 84, 86, 87
ad hominem attacks, 164
Aeschylus, 20
Africa, 143
African Americans, 42, 70
African history, 26–27, 66, 119 ff., 135, 141, 173
African National Congress, 90–94, 141
Africanism, in South Africa, 92, 93
Africans, 42, 61; overseas, 102, 146
Afrikaans (language), 94
Afrocentrism, 27, 131, 132, 141
Afrocentricity, 94
Agard, Walter, R., 19, 21, 24, 27, 51
Ailred of Rievaulx, 22–23, 24
Aladura Churches (Nigeria), 63
American (United States) history, 146–147, 172
Amis, Kingsley, 22
Ancient Near East
Angevin Empire, 24
Anglo-Saxon dominance, 42
Anselm, Saint, 23, 24
Apartheid (South Africa), 82, 83, 91, 92, 93, 115, 141, 176
apologetics, 120, 121
    of difference, 127;
    of equivalence, 127;
    of precedence, 130 ff.
Appiah, Kwame Anthony, 178
Aristophanes, 19
Asante (West African kingdom), 98, 125
Asante, Molefi Kete, 7

assimilation, 10, 144
audience, 47, 48, 53
Auschwitz, 46
Australia, 71, 155
Austria, 74
authenticity, 43, 50, 135 ff., 141
authority (in classroom), 150, 159
automobiles, 157
Azanian Peoples' Organization (AZAPO), 93

balance, 83, 164, 165, 166
baseline, 18, 122, 124, 125, 128, 129
be-bop, 77
Becker, Carl L., 21, 42
Belgium, 53
benign power (as not-imperialism), 100
Berkeley, University of California at, 17, 180
bias, 1, 31, 59, 84, 159, 165, 174
Biko, Steve, 92
biological insiderism, 43
biological race, 114–116
Bisoondath, Neil, 176
Black Consciousness (in South Africa), 85, 92
Black Studies, 27
Bloom, Allan, 7
Bondurant, Joan, 37
Booth, Philip, 65
Botha, P. W., 93
Botha reforms, 93
Botswana, 103
boycott (of Apartheid South Africa), 89–90
Brahmins, 14
Brazil, 74
Brentano, Robert, 22–24, 27, 30, 51

Brink, Andre, 178
Brinton, Crane, 78
Britain, 53, 176
Brzezinski, Zbigniew, 78
Burns, Sir Alan, 119
Brutus, Dennis, 89

Calabar, 98
Calcutta, 176
Canada, 71, 107, 143
Canon, 6, 7–8, 173
Cape Colony (South Africa), 103
Cape liberalism, 91
Caribbean, 176
cartography, 37–38
catchment, 110
censorship, 13
Cesaire, Aime, 126, 127
Cetshwayo (Zulu king), 99
Ceylon, 156 (*see also*, Sri Lanka)
Chalk, Frank, 76
China, 179
Chinese, overseas, 102, 146
Christ, 23
chronological foreshortening, 32, 56
chronological history, 149–150,
    153, 160
Cleopatra, 130
Cold War, 24
collaborators, 54–55, 56
colleaguiality, 28
colonial rule, 54
colonialism, 73
colonizer-colonized dichotomy, 32,
    53 ff., 90, 104, 143
Columbus, Christopher, 101
communalism, 111, 112, 145, 148
comparative history, 65 ff., 156
    (*see also*, comparison)
comparison, 2, 65 ff., 166–167
    of connected cases, 74
    invidious, 75, 166
    between South Africa and the
        United States, 69–70, 89–90
computer learning, 172

concepts, 73, 106, 157, 159
Congo, Belgian, 63
Congress Alliance, 92 (*see also*,
    African National Congress)
connotations, 107–109
Conservative Party (South Africa), 4
conservatives, 7–8, 17–18, 23, 149
Cortez, 99
counterfactual reasoning, 101, 157
cultural arrogance, 91
cultural nationalism, 55, 59–60
Cultural Revolution (China), 179
culture wars, 1, 14
curriculum, controversy over, 7, 8,
    18, 19, 24, 147–148
Curtin, Philip D., 3, 25–27, 51. 69,
    71–71
Curtis, Edward, 137–138
Cyprus, 9
Czechoslovakia, 179

Dahl, Robert A., 10
deconstruction, 18
degree, statements of, 67, 72
de Kiewiet, Cornelis W., 68, 70–71
demography, 102–103
Dennis, Carl, 143
Desai, Anita, 177
Dike, K. Onwuke, 119
Diop, Cheikh Anta, 121
disciplines, academic, 154
discovery classroom, 150
discussion, 6, 22, 50, 105, 106,
    107, 117, 127, 161, 163 ff.
    (*see also*, rules of discussion,
    documents)
diversity, 1, 11, 12, 13, 31, 144,
    147, 151, 173
divide and rule, 56, 145, 146
documents, analysis of in
    classroom, 6, 22, 86, 103–104,
    127, 132, 136, 138, 139,
    141–142, 155
Drabble, Margaret, 177
D'Souza, Dinesh, 7, 12, 14, 137, 138

Dube, Ernest, 81
Dumas, Henry, 41, 46
Dunn, Stephen, 53
Durham, Lord, 143

Eastern Europe, 143
Egypt, Ancient, 130, 131, 132
Elkins, Stanley, 76
English language, 94
epidemiology, 102
ethnocentrism, 22, 32–33, 174
Euripides, 20
Eurocentrism, 48, 103
Europeans, as migrants, 102
examinations, 31, 151, 165–166
Experimental College (at University
    of Wisconsin), 19

facts, 29–30, 71, 106, 128, 152,
    154, 157, 159, 160, 172
fact-value dichotomy, 128
Fanon, Frantz, 59, 62, 137
Farrakahn, Louis, 89
Feiermann, Steven, 136
Fiji, 9
Finley, Moses I., 74
Fish, Stanley, 7
Fo, Dario, 179
formalism, (style of economic
    analysis), 127–128
France, 53
Fredrickson, George M., 14, 67–68,
    69
free trade (as not-imperialism),
    99–100
Freedom Charter (South Africa), 90,
    93, 94
Freedom Struggle (South Africa), 89 ff.
Fuentes, Carlo, 179

Gallagher, John, 100
Gandhi, Mohandas K., 35, 39, 86
    (see also, Gandhian truth)
Gandhian truth, 15, 35–36, 39, 51,
    102, 127, 132, 142, 174

Gay Studies, 18
Gellner, Ernest, 109, 110
genocide, 76, 144
Germans, 42
Ghosh, Amitav, 176
Gordimer, Nadine, 177
Gordon, Sir Arthur, 74
Graves, Robert, 81, 87
great community, 126
Great Trek (South Africa), 141
Greece, ancient, 130
    democracy in, 20
Guatemala, 138, 139
Guggisberg, Gov. Gordon, 125

Hadas, Rachel, 180
Halley's Comet, 140
Hancock, Sir William Keith, 25–26,
    68, 71, 98
Hapsburg Empire, 100
Harvard University, 25
Hilferding, Rudolf, 98
hindsight bias, 32, 54 (see also, bias)
Hoffman, Daniel, 149
holocause, 76
Honesty, King Eyo (Calabar), 98
Hulm, Keri, 176
Husein, Taha, 177

imperial rule, 145
imperialism, 2, 45, 73, 97 ff., 156,
    158, 173
    cultural, 42, 94
    intellectual, 48
Indians, 42
    overseas, 102, 146
India, British, 53
Indochina, French, 53
Indonesia, 9, 53, 77
inquiry, 83
inquiry classroom, 150
insider-outsider contrast, 41 ff.
insiderism, 27, 43, 167, 173–174
Integrated Liberal Studies (ILS),
    University of Wisconsin, 18–19

intensity, statements of, 72
Iranian Revolution, 78
Iranians, 42
Irish, 42
Isandhlwana, battle of, 1879, 99
Islam, 81
Islamic nationalism, 111

Jameson, Storm, 176–177
Jervois, Sir William, 74
Johnson, J. C. de Graft, 121
Johnson, Samuel (Yoruba historian),
    119
Jonassohn, Kurt, 76

Kaufman, Shirley, 163
Kautsky, Karl, 98
Keegan, Tim, 136, 137
Kemal, Yashar, 177
Kenyatta, Jomo, 48
Khama (King of Ngwato), 103
Kimball, Roger, 7
Kimbanguist churches, 63
Kincaid, Jamaica, 137
Kivnick, Helen, 89–90, 94
Kolko, Gabriel, 77
Kundera, Milan, 177, 178, 179
Kuti, Ransome, 176

Lamarckian theory, 108
Latino studies, 18
Lebanon, 9
Leed, Eric J., 46
Lembede, Anton, 92
Lenin, 98
Levant, 143
Levi, Primo, 46
Life, 19
liberalism, 5, 28, 115, 116, 145, 154
little community, 126
location, 158
London, 176
Luxemburg, Rosa, 98

MacArthur Fellowship, 25
McLuhan, Marshall, 38

McNeill, William, 131, 158
Malaya, 9, 156
Mandela, Maki, 89, 94–95
Mandela, Nelson, 89, 91, 92, 93
manifest destiny, 100
manipulative collaboration, 63
map projections, 37
Maoris, 103–104
Marxism, 112, 115, 116
mazeway, 75
Meiklejohn, Alexander, 19, 21–22
Melian dialogue (Thucydides), 20
Memmi, Albert, 48
Menchu, Rigoberta, 137, 138
mercantilism, 99
Meredith, William, 29
migration, 102–103
Miles, Josephine, 2, 77, 135, 171, 180
Milner, Lord, 108
mindset, 31, 57, 151
mishmash, 38
Modisane, Bloke, 45, 46
Mongols, 14
Montreal Institute for Genocide
    Studies, 76
Moore, Brian, 177
multiculturalism, 10, 173
Mzilikazi (Ndebele king), 140

Naipaul, V. S., 177
nation-building, 120
National Defense Education Act, 24
National Party (South Africa), 91
nationalism, 2, 73, 100, 105 ff., 157
Native Americans, 42, 70
Native American studies, 18
New Zealand, 103, 176, 179
    history of, 2
Nazi Germany, 66
Nehru, Jawaharlal, 144, 146
Nene, Tamati Waka, 103
neocolonialism, 129
neo-Hinduism, 77
neo-traditionalism, 61
Ngugi wa-Thiongo, 177, 178
Ngwato (people of Botswana), 103

Nigeria, 63, 176
Nkrumah, Kwame, 125

open classroom, 150, 154
Opoku Ware (Asante king), 175
orientalism, 48
others, the other, 111–112, 135 ff., 174
outsiders, 43–44, 61, 112–113, 117, 136 (*see also*, insider-outsider contrast)

Pacific region, 143
pain, 45
Pan Africanist Congress (PAC), 92, 93
Pakistan, 111
partition (of territory), 144
Pericles, 19
periodization, 157
Phillips, Caryl, 176
pioneer settlement, 100
Plaatje, Sol, 94, 140, 141
platonic theory, 153
plural societies, 156
pluralism, 9, 11–12, 143 ff.
  in higher education, 147
pluralist classroom, 149 ff., 161
political correctness, 6, 7, 173
Pope Hennessy, Sir John, 74
positivism, 37, 7273, 168, 172, 174
poststructuralism, 18
Prague, 179
presentism, 22, 120
Punjab, 10
Puritans, 42

questions, 15, 152, 153, 172

race question (in Canada and South Africa), 107
race relations, 156
racism, 2, 45, 13, 45, 56, 73, 81, 85, 86, 105 ff., 130–131, 145, 154, 157
  as basis for group loyalty, 114
  definition of, 113–114

radicals, 8, 18
Ranger, Terence, 62
reading, critical skills in, 2, 84, 121, 130, 139–140, 142, 153, 154, 155, 159, 175 ff.
reciprocity, 128
redistribution, 128
reformers (in colonial societies), 57–59
reification, 60
relativism, 21, 32–33, 36, 40, 50, 174
  and ethnocentrism, 35
  objections to, 34
resistance-collaboration dichotomy, 55, 57
Rhodes, Cecil, 103
Rieff, Philip, 84
Rivonia Trial Statement (by Nelson Mandela), 91
Robben Island, 93
Robinson, Ronald, 100
Rorty, Richard, 174
rules of discussion, 2, 50, 163 ff.

Samkange, Stanlake, 177
satyagraha, 35
Savelle, Max, 20
Sayles, G. O., 24
Schevill, James, 17, 180
Scott, Dennis, 97, 104
secularism, 144
self-assessment, 41 ff., 49 ff.
separatism (ethnic), 11
Setswana (language), 94
Shakespeare, William, 94
Sierra Leone, 74
Simmel, Georg, 47
slave trade, 71–72
slavery, 76
Sobukwe, Robert, 92
social race, 114–116
Socrates, 19
solidarity, 174
Sophocles, 19

South Africa, 107, 115
  history of, 39, 66, 69–70, 81 ff.,
    89 ff., 148, 173
South Asia, 143
Southeast Asia, 143
Soyinka, Wole, 176
span, 25–26, 75
speech codes, 6, 7, 12, 13
Spitzer, Leo, 74
Sri Lanka, 9, 10, 177
stereotypes, 33–34, 112
Stimpson, Catharine, 7
Stony Brook, State University of
  New York at, 82, 84, 143
student audience, 29 ff.
substantivist view, 127
Sudan, Western, 126
Swarthmore College, 25
symbolic resistance, 63

tabula rasa, theory of learning, 150
Tanzania, 93
temperament of teacher, 49
territorial state, 158
Third World, 3, 104, 141, 174
Thornton, A. P. 100–101
Thucydides, 20
timing, 158
Toronto, 176
total institutions, 76
tradition, 60–61, 113
traditional classroom, 150–151
traditional-modern dichotomy, 55,
  57
traditionalism, 60 (*see also*,
  neo-traditionalism)
trans-Mississippi West, 156
Trevelyan, G. M., 23, 24
tribalism, 111, 112, 123
Trinidad, 176
Turks, 14

uhuru, 123, 125
ujamaa, 123, 126
United Democratic Front (South
  Africa), 93, 94
United States, 71, 155, 177
  history of, 69–70, 159

value-fact distinction, 106, 107
Vargas Llosa, Mario, 177, 179
Vietnam war, 17, 21, 22
Vinz, Mark, 1
violence, 61–62
Vonnegut, Kurt, Jr., 178

Waddell, Hope, 98
Waitangi, Treaty of, 103–104
Washington, University of, 20, 30
West African history, 2
West Germany, 46
westernization, 58
Westminster model, 125
westward expansion, in United
  States history, 100–101
WHA (Wisconsin public
  broadcasting service), 19
White Australia, 71
Wilbur, Richard, 105
Williams, Chancellor, 121
Wisconsin, University of, 17, 18,
  24–25
Witwatersrand Oral Documentation
  Project, 136
women's studies, 18
Woolf, Leonard, 177
writing assignments, 175

Yang, Jiang, 179
Yoruba, 119

Zionism, 81
Zulu, 14